Ending the Battle Within

Ending the Battle Within

Verlaine Crawford

High Castle Publishing

For information address:

High Castle Publishing
P.O. Box 3038
Idyllwild, CA 92549
Phone: (909) 659-3594
Fax: (909) 659-4164

FIRST EDITION: September 1994

SECOND PRINTING: May 1995

Distributed in the United States by Atrium Distributors

Cover Design by Lightbourne Images, Ashland, OR

Printed and Bound by Delta Lithograph, Valencia, CA

Library of Congress Cataloging in Publication Data

Crawford, Verlaine, 1943-
    Ending the Battle Within: How to Create a Harmonious Life
    by Working With Your Sub-Personalities
    1. Psychology. 2. Self-help. 3. New Age movement 4. Health
I. Title.

ISBN 0-96-418540-7

Dedication
to Louise Hay

How would you describe greatness? Is it fame, fortune or power? There are many descriptions, but I would like to define greatness as touching people's lives in a positive way. Louise Hay has positively changed lives through the sale of over three million books and through her wonderful tapes and personal appearances. She has helped individuals to heal their minds, bodies and souls. She has been a powerful inspiration for many seekers on the path for truth. Her insight and wisdom has been a guiding light through the darkness of confusion for countless individuals, including myself. Thank you, Louise, for helping me and all the people you have touched.

MESSAGE FROM LOUISE HAY

We all know how hard it is to change our negative patterns, mainly because we do not know what it is inside of us that really needs changing. Verlaine Crawford has come up with a simple but most effective way of learning *who* really dwells within us. There are far more sub-personalities than we are aware of. Her Infusion Integration Technique helps us make peace with them once and for all. Verlaine is living proof that her process can turn lives around as she continues to expand the boundaries of her own life.

Students in America and around the world are benefiting from her workshops. This book is a must read for all who are serious about changing their lives for the better. This will also be the most fun growth experience you have ever had.

I wish Verlaine had written this book years ago when I was beginning my own journey.

Louise Hay, author of
You Can Heal Your Life

Contents

Foreword

Can there be a new way of healing the mind, body and emotions? Every few years a new concept enters the healing profession and helps us to gain a new perspective on providing insights and improving the quality of people's lives. Most recently, working with the inner child has gained popularity and the concept of the child-like part-of-us needing nurturing and protection has helped many people to heal past memories, thus becoming more spontaneous and joyful in their lives.

Ending the Battle Within presents the Infusion Integration Technique which has all the ingredients of a new and powerful tool that can help to reprogram the mind and change the inner dynamics of personality, thus affecting one's interaction with life experiences and relationships with others.

Traditional western medical practices are now going through profound changes as individuals explore new methods of self-development. Looking closely at the idea that we are each a composite of ever-shifting sub-personalities holding onto old concepts and beliefs which create our life activities, relationships, and even disease in the body is a valuable and revolutionary concept.

If we conclude that our thoughts actually affect our environment, moving us into the world to create what we desire and what we fear, then we would be wise to examine those thoughts and know what we are thinking, believing and holding as "truisms" within us.

If the universe and all within it are in the process of creation, then there can be no absolute future. As creative beings we need not be unwilling puppets following the dictates of some imaginary pre-written life script. We can claim our free will, determine our experiences and life direction through our own thoughts and actions and be guided by our expanded understanding of the factors influencing individual manifestation.

Ending the Battle Within serves as both a textbook and a workbook allowing you to participate in self-discovery exercises that can open your mind and heart to who you are and help you release the blocks to manifesting your heart's desires. Once you grasp the concept of sub-personalities and how to harmonize the various parts-of-you with the Infusion Integration Technique, you will have an opportunity to experience a fuller understanding of your complexity and potential. This inner exploration is truly of greater importance than the outer exploration of the universe will ever be to mankind. The Infusion Integration Technique leads to a sense of confident inner peace and the experience of seemingly divine magic, allowing us to meet life's challenges with a feeling of purpose and adventure in place of the battle within.

Through many years as a practicing psychiatrist, I have treated thousands of patients in the throes of intense pain and confusion. I have seen how thoughts can lead individuals down dark alleys of depression and into the agitation of anxiety. People who are suffering through painful problems should not be afraid or ashamed to seek professional guidance. There are times that we all can gain considerably by sharing our problems openly with someone who has been trained to help us unravel the mysteries of our minds.

For those of you who are able and willing to read *Ending the Battle Within*, do the exercises and write the new scenario of your life, you have a rare and wonderful opportunity to learn to examine your thoughts and actions, and to see how "magical coincidences" can occur which bring you closer to your heart's desires. You can learn to see each of your experiences as a beacon of light illuminating your underlying thoughts and beliefs, showing you who you are and what you believe. And best of all, you can change your thoughts and beliefs. You can alter the decisions that have formed negative patterns and emotions in your life.

Verlaine takes us on a journey of discovery through her own life experiences and the challenges she met with people she has worked with over the past twenty years. She allows us to view her own struggle and her emergence into a new way of living in peace, harmony, joy and abundance.

You have before you a grand adventure, a journey into the unknown of what is possible in your life. Drink deeply and fully, allowing yourself to see, feel and live your wildest dreams. Release yourself to the joy of unveiling who you truly are. Learn about the amazing solutions available within the inner creative part-of-you. Reading this book, you can end the emotional battle within. You can free your heart and mind and find inner peace. Prepare the canvas of your life and begin to paint your heart's desires.

Thomas B. Jackson, M.D.
Chief Psychiatrist
Director of Research
Tri-City Mental Health Center
Pomona, California

Preface

Over the past seven years, I have had the opportunity to teach the Infusion Integration Technique through workshops and seminars around the world. I have used this process to work with individuals and groups in California, the Midwest and New York, Paris, London, Hong Kong, Tokyo and Osaka, Japan, and Sidney and Melbourne, Australia. I have appeared on television and radio and met with many audiences.

As I have traveled the world, the warmth, love and hospitality I have received have brought me a feeling of fulfillment beyond whatever I dreamed possible. I have often been asked to write a book about the Infusion Integration Technique and to include the many stories that I tell as I lead groups and individuals into a new discovery of who they are and what they might accomplish in their lives. Hopefully, this book will reach the many people who are searching for answers to the eternal question "How can I make my life more harmonious, fun, abundant and fulfilled?"

I often speak of the four cornerstones of life: health, wealth, love and self-expression. If any of these four foundation stones are missing, the structure of your life begins to tilt. Unless all four major ingredients of life are working for you, your life may tend to be out of balance.

It has been stated in a variety of self-help books that we create our reality. Yet many people who have worked long and hard on perfecting their affirmations and planting positive thoughts in their minds, often manifest pain and difficulty in their lives. Through my search over the past twenty-five years to discover how we create our reality, I have uncovered some important answers and perfected helpful tools that have resulted in my learning how to manifest my wildest dreams and live in a nearly continuous state of peacefulness. Because my own life is now so lovely, I feel confident sharing the techniques and tools that I have practiced with myself and with others to gain positive, effective results. Lives have frequently been changed almost overnight, and it is my pleasure to share this information with you.

In my own life journey, my early years were spent living in a country home with a view of the Mississippi River near LeClaire, Iowa. At the age of sixteen, my family and I moved to Carmel, California, where I graduated from high school in 1962. I then attended the University of California at Berkeley, majoring in Political Science and International Relations.

From 1967 to 1975, I held a variety of jobs. I was editor of *Keynotes* magazine at Capitol Records, then publicist for the Queen Mary project, the civic light opera and the Olympic tryouts in Long Beach. I enjoyed being editor of six weekly newspapers in the San Gabriel Valley, chief copywriter for an advertising agency in Los Angeles and director of a chamber of commerce on the Monterey Peninsula.

From 1975 to 1980, I was sales director for the Lodge at Pebble Beach, enjoying the excitement of helping to make arrangements for many top corporate and political visitors. In 1980, I formed my own marketing business in the San Francisco Bay Area, doing public relations and advertising for a variety of clients, including national promotional projects for large corporations. From 1982 to 1987, I was vice president of marketing and sales and co-founder of two computer software firms in Silicon Valley.

In January 1987, I experienced the next major change in my life. I felt as if I was tapped on the shoulder and a voice said to me, "You've marketed many things, now market the idea that your thoughts create your reality." I had been working diligently to make this seemingly simple concept work in my life, and it usually had proved very successful. I decided to find a way to help individuals to move into alignment with their thoughts and life patterns.

My quest to understand the meaning of life and how we create our reality began twenty years before in March 1967. I was riding in a rickety, old elevator in the apartment building where I was renting a small studio in Los Angeles. A man in the elevator started talking to me. "You look sad," he said.

"You're right. Things are not great in my life," I replied.

He introduced himself as Dave and started to explain to me that there was a way I could take control of my life. He suggested I make a list of the things I wanted and write down the dates by which they would happen. He told me an amazing story of how making a list of his desires had worked for him.

A year before, Dave had been a drunken bum sitting on the sidewalk on Sixth Street in Los Angeles. He had lost all his money and property through a set of terrible circumstances. A well-dressed man came walking toward Dave and sat down next to him on the street. The stranger told Dave that he could change his life. He suggested that Dave make a list of the things he wanted and write next to each item the date he wanted them to happen. Dave had literally nothing to lose so he made the list. He wrote that he would own an office building on Wilshire Boulevard by a certain date; he would be driving a new, white Thunderbird convertible by another date; and he would move into a penthouse apartment on Wilshire by the last date.

"Everything has happened!" he exclaimed. "I've got all that I wrote on the list, and each thing happened before the dates I had written." He proceeded to take me on a short ride in his new Thunderbird and showed me around his office building and his beautiful penthouse apartment that he was to move into the following week.

He continued talking about how this was such an amazing phenomenon and that he was busy working on his second list as we drove back to my old apartment building. We rode the elevator up to my floor.

"Make your list!" he called to me as I walked toward my apartment. Once inside, the strangeness of this encounter began to fade as I thought about my problems.

My thoughts were interrupted by a knock on the door. "Now what?" I asked myself.

As I opened the door, Dave handed me a book, *As a Man Thinketh*, by James Allen. "Read this book and make your list," he called out to me, as he hurried down the hallway. I never saw Dave again. Those few moments changed my life.

I decided to make an outrageous list. Why not? The whole idea seemed so silly.

The list I wrote was as follows:

- I will be modeling by April 15. (I was taking fashion design classes but didn't think I was pretty enough to be a model.)
- I will appear on television by May 20. (I didn't even own a television.)
- I will be living in an apartment at the beach for $110 per month by June 1. (This was cheap rent even in 1967.)
- I will be driving a Jaguar XKE on my birthday in December. (I owned a five-year-old, beat-up Volkswagen at the time.)

Everything happened without my working on the list. I didn't try to figure out how I could make these things appear in my life. I certainly had no great faith in the process. I didn't think about what I had written. I simply put the list in my desk drawer and forgot about it. Soon, amazing coincidences began to occur. My intuition led me in strange ways.

A few days after writing the list, I heard a young couple, sitting next to me in a restaurant, talking about acting tryouts being held at Capitol Records in Hollywood for an off-Broadway play, *The Fountainhead* by Ayn Rand. The book had impressed me when I read it in college. I decided to try out for the lead role, just for the fun of it. (I had appeared in a play in the eighth grade and hadn't acted since. I just felt it would be interesting to meet the people who were involved with such a play.)

The interviewer took one look at me and said, "I'm sorry, you're too young for the part. Why do you want to be an actress?"

"I don't really want to be an actress. I want to be a writer," I replied.

"Oh, okay," she said as she left the room. She returned a few minutes later with the President of the Capitol Records Club, which published a magazine called *Keynotes.*

He asked me if I would like to work on the magazine, and I replied, joyfully, "Yes, I'd love to." I took the job of assistant editor, and my life began to change for the better.

One month later, the Creative Director asked me if I would like to model in one of the ads in the magazine. I accepted and found myself modeling. (I didn't ask for the cover of *Vogue.*)

Two weeks later a friend who sold insurance called and asked if I would like to be on television. It was a pilot for a computer dating game. I wouldn't be paid, but I would be treated to dinner at the Magic Castle, a private club in the Hollywood Hills. I was thrilled. I'd always wanted to go to the Magic Castle (where magicians put on great shows). And I saw myself on television. (I didn't ask for a hit series or my own talk show.)

Two items on the list had happened! I was shocked and excited to realize the list was working. I decided it was time to find the apartment at the beach. When I told my Mom I was going to look for an apartment, she asked me if I was going to search through the newspapers.

"No. I'm going to drive north from Newport Beach and hope that my intuition will lead me to it," I replied with a new confidence and excitement.

I drove along the ocean and came to the lovely inlets and islands of Belmont Shores, south of Long Beach. I rounded a curve and saw a sandy, white beach on an inland waterway. There was a sign: "Apartment For Rent." I rented the two-room, furnished apartment for $110 per month. The walls were natural pine and there were sunlit windows overlooking a garden and the beach.

Yes, I was driving a yellow XKE Jaguar on my birthday. It belonged to the man I began dating at the time. He asked me if I wanted to drive on the way to my birthday dinner. He didn't know about the list. (I had written I would be driving the XKE, not owning it.)

I analyzed everything that had happened—all the coincidences, which had seemed to appear. I was intrigued and began a life-long investigation.

From that year forward, I adopted the quest of discovering how thoughts become reality. As each item or event would happen in my life, I would piece together the puzzle of how it came into being. What were the thoughts I had been thinking? What were the feelings or intuition which came into play? How did the events develop? As I watched many stories unfold, I could see that the ability to manifest appeared to be related to following one's intuition.

Over the next ten years, I wrote many lists and watched my desires manifest. I changed my life, and watched other people change their lives by making lists of what they wanted. Some of the wonderful stories of large and small miracles are told throughout this book.

But questions kept arising. Though many of the results of making lists had been miraculous, not all of the manifestations developed as my friends and I had listed. Why was this technique successful sometimes, but not at others? I began seeking the answer to this question and searched many years for the solution to this mystery.

In 1977, I attended a series of fascinating classes in Carmel called the Laws of Health, Wealth and Manifestation. Through the classes, I started to understand the "how" of creation. I discovered that thoughts, activated by emotion, are like packets of energy, which flow from us to other people, creating what we desire and what we fear. A year later, I learned the Infusion Integration Technique, which finally illuminated the underlying dynamics of the more subtle and mysterious aspects of successfully manifesting our heart's desires.

I became aware that what we consciously desire can be in direct conflict with subconscious elements of our personalities that resist and undermine what we want to manifest. I discovered the complexity of our subconscious mind, which seems to be made up of sub-personalities with their own well-defined desires, fears and resistances. The challenge became finding the techniques to communicate with our sub-personalities, heal their fears and out-dated concepts (often left over from early childhood experience), and create a harmonious consensus in order to clear the way for manifesting our most important desires. The evaluation of this approach resulted in the development of the Infusion Integration Technique, which you will learn through what I hope will be an adventure reading this book.

During the 1980s, as I worked in the business world, I used the Infusion Integration Technique and shared it with others to help in the manifestation of our goals and desires. I have tested the technique with hundreds of people and have been amazed by how consistently people achieve dramatic results. Infusion has served as a powerful tool that has assisted me in living a joyous, peaceful and fulfilling life. It often takes time, concentration and dedication to change your life. You are worth the effort. Why not begin now?

Introduction

Of all the beautiful truths pertaining to the soul
which have been restored and brought to light in this age,
none is more gladdening or fruitful of divine promise
and confidence than this—that I am the master of my thought,
the molder of my character, and the maker
and shaper of my condition, environment, and destiny.

James Allen, *As a Man Thinketh*

For some of you this book may seem very basic. It might seem so easy, so simplistic—the idea that you can learn to live, to laugh, to love by changing your mind. The possibility that you really can create your own reality and live it abundantly is perhaps a strange concept to some, but to others of us who have witnessed our own inner changes, followed by outer changes, we know we can alter our lives.

I have seen my outer landscape of life reflect my inner battle-ground. I have worked with my various sub-personalities to create an inner peace. I have witnessed my outer life turn into a mountain Shangri-La with terraced gardens of glorious flowers overlooking pine forest-covered peaks and the ever-changing play of clouds, light and color upon the mountainside. I have confirmed for myself that my outer world reflects and feeds back to me what I am holding as my inner thoughts and beliefs.

I know that each of our lives can be our greatest work of art. We are the creators and formers of a multi-dimensional destiny filled with infinite probabilities. We can let the programming that we have lived through childhood, adolescence and adulthood affect us, or we can take the reins of the runaway carriage that we call our lives. We can calm the horses and steer a clear course to our desired destinations.

The past is a phantom that no longer needs to haunt you. You no longer need to delve deeply into a subconscious that is believed to be filled only with muck and mire. Instead, you can discover in your subconscious a hidden reserve of wisdom, power, and, yes, love that can sustain you. You can learn to appreciate the power of the present in each moment and release the visions of past drama and trauma, which can build vacuums in your vision quest for a greater, more wholesome and peaceful life.

My experience of this lifetime is a feeling of having lived so fully that my time on earth seems equivalent to many different lives, each with their own death and rebirth. At one point in 1990, after I had lost everything I held dear, and had finally surrendered to God, I felt time move slower and slower until it seemed to nearly stop. For many weeks, I could feel long pauses between people speaking their sentences, even between their words. I had no thoughts to interrupt the quiet I felt between the staccato sentences of friends, co-workers and passersby. It was a great freedom, a tremendous relief to be free from the demands of various sub-personalities who had argued for control of my life. There were no more needs, wants or desires. I was free to fly easily in a pure blue sky and to dance lightly with the graceful flight of the butterfly.

What I felt was beyond all the rewards of my liberated woman's success in the business world and the associated acknowledgment. I'd made my point, and finally I had chosen freedom rather than restraint. Love, peace and relaxation superseded power, prestige and exhaustion.

I wrote this book to let you know there is a method, a tool that can help you reprogram your mind. I call it the Infusion Integration Technique. In Webster's Dictionary, *infusionism* is defined as that moment when spirit enters form. I maintain that infusionism is a process. Your body and mind is being re-created every moment by a continuous flow of energy from your soul. Your soul needs room to breathe—a space of quiet and reserve energy—in order to function effectively in form. When you integrate opposing beliefs held by your sub-personalities, you allow your mind to relax and become quiet.

You can achieve this sense of quietness by understanding what is causing the noise. What is driving you? What are you thinking about when you blank out for miles while driving on the freeway? Where are you as you rush from one appointment to another?

What do you really want out of life? What would you do if money were no object? Who are you anyway? What would you ask for if suddenly a genie appeared in front of you saying, "Yes, I will grant you three wishes"?

It doesn't take long to sit down and consider what you would prefer to have in your life. Yet most people don't even take five minutes to write down their preferences. Most people take more time considering their grocery lists than they do considering where they would really like to live, what type of person they would like to live with, and what they would really, truly like to do with their time—to earn a living and to create a beautiful life.

You normally wouldn't even consider going grocery shopping without some sort of list, yet you walk forward each day without knowing your heart's desires, the dreams you would love to manifest and the joys you would love to discover.

This is it. The time has come for many of us to reevaluate who we are and what we want to do with the time remaining for us on earth. No one knows for certain how long we have to live. It could be a day, a week, months or many years. So it is important to realize that each day can represent a complete lifetime as the sun rises and sets. Each moment may be enjoyed with a true appreciation of the beauty and harmony of the life process. We can choose to see the flowers growing along the roadside when we are caught in traffic, or we can pretend we are caught in a war zone and engaged in combat. Each moment we have the opportunity to choose love or fear, peace or battle. Sometimes the choice is between being happy or right.

The battle begins inside of each one of us. If there is no battle inside, we will experience no battle outside. It is a strange and wonderful phenomenon, this biofeedback system called life in form. What you feel inside is what you get outside.

The purpose of this book is to help further the understanding of this feedback phenomenon. Over the past twenty-five years I have tested the theories of Infusion on myself and hundreds of other people. I know that the changes I discuss are possible, for I have lived them.

It has been said, "Know thyself." Know who you are and you will know the reasons for your life. You will understand the meaning of what has happened to you. You will be able to access the knowledge you have gained from all of your experiences. You will be able to put yourself directly in charge of your life. You will be aware of the smallest nuances of your thought processes, since your thoughts are being shown to you in living color on the big screen of your life each day. And you will be able to turn the channel and write a new scenario for your life, one that appeals to you now. You can change that scenario again, if you want to, and again and again. You can create endless scenarios as you live day to day and experience the creative process called living in form.

THE UNIVERSE PROVIDES MAGICAL WAYS TO CREATE YOUR DREAMS

I would rather be least among men
with dreams and the desire to fulfill them,
than the greatest among men
with no dreams and no desires.

Kahlil Gibran

For people with a scientific orientation, the theories in this book may require the suspension of normal logic. It may be necessary to be open to new concepts, such as "Our thoughts really can create our reality," in order to enjoy a more enriching and exciting way of life.

Any knowledgeable scientist who understands the nature of perception and how the mind works is aware that we truly do create our own subjective reality. The sights, smells, colors, sounds and sensations that seem to emanate from outside of us, in fact, are solely and completely creations within our own minds. Our sensory nerves, which allow us to hear, see and feel, are stimulated by waves of sounds and light or by direct touch at the surface of the skin. These sensations are sent via nerves to the brain, where impressions are then interpreted and perception created.

An example of our interpreted reality is the fact that there is no color red outside of the brain. The visual sensations of the colors in a sunset are simply a picture created inside your own mind. The feeling of joy you experience as you listen to an outdoor orchestra, with a cool evening breeze blowing softly against your face, is in actuality no more than impulses of nerves flowing into your brain where the experience is created. What you perceive becomes your personal reality.

Is it really any more wondrous or amazing that we might be able to influence external events occurring around us, than the fact that we totally create the internal experiences of those events?

FEELING AND DESIRE

The purpose of the creative exercises in this book is to help you get in touch with the feelings you want to experience. If, by using a picture of an item or a person or by imagining a place, you are able to bring about the feeling you desire, then use it. But don't confuse the item, the material manifestation, with the feeling you want. Don't place the physical experience above the joy you wish to feel.

It is important to be on the lookout for the novel ways which the universe has of providing these feelings and experiences. Many people are so caught up in physical goals they forget the feelings they want to experience. They decide owning a house, a certain car or a boat is what will make them happy. The item itself can be wonderful, but the most important ingredient necessary to manifest what you want is to concentrate on the feeling of happiness you desire.

For example, at one time I thought it would be fun to own a yacht, a very big yacht, moored at Cannes in the South of France. I used the technique described later in this book, "See it, feel it, be it, sense the source and expect magical fulfillment."

I imagined (saw in my mind's eye) a beautiful 100-foot yacht anchored offshore. I walked on deck in my mind and saw the lovely decor: sea mist green and peach pillows, polished wood and brass. There were great displays of fruit, seafood, champagne and flowers laid out for the guests. I saw myself going to the captain's wheel and steering the yacht out to the islands.

I felt deeply the experience of being on the yacht, the soft breeze, the slickness of the wood, the excitement of being out on the open sea.

Then I became the yacht. I imagined what it would be like to be that huge mass of wood and metal, floating on the waves, receiving "oohs" and "ahs" from my guests.

I sensed the source, the energy that created the yacht, the same energy that creates all things, and I let the idea float out of my mind toward its fulfillment.

Did I manifest a yacht? Yes. I was able to have a wonderful afternoon and evening on a gorgeous yacht in Fort Lauderdale, Florida, as a guest of American Telephone and Telegraph, when I was vice president of a software company. The yacht was huge, and the colors matched those in my imagination. There was seafood, fruit, champagne and rock and roll music playing, and we danced as we cruised through the island waterways.

Did I own the yacht? No. And I did not need to purchase the boat or pay for the mooring fees or upkeep of the yacht. I simply enjoyed the feeling I had imagined as I lived the experience. It is possible to enjoy an event so much that you really don't feel the need to repeat it. Owning a yacht might have been nice, but it really didn't fit into my lifestyle, so I was delighted to manifest the feeling I had practiced in my mind.

When you are only in tune with one aspect of your personality, you may think you want to become rich, so you may have a beautiful home, furniture, cars, etc. When you are attuned to all aspects of your personality, you may discover you would still like to be rich and it would still be desirable to have a nice house and car. Yet, in addition to the physical manifestation of your desires, your whole self may wish to begin assisting other people and help to heal the planet. You may find avenues of expression that you would not have considered in the past.

As you clarify and integrate your sub-personalities, you will be able to find peace, direction and consistency. You can set your true course, which usually turns out to be some greater purpose for your life. When coincidences begin to occur, you can rejoice as you become involved in miraculous and synchronous events that will support you in reaching your goals.

CHAPTER 1

Our Selves Are Tearing Us Apart

The map is not the territory,
but if you don't know where you're going,
and you don't know
what you would like to see when you get there,
then no map can take you—
because you aren't going anywhere.

In all of recorded history there have been reports of individuals making a breakthrough in consciousness and suddenly realizing their wholeness, their oneness with God or the universe. Upon the doorways of ancient temples is written the inscription "Know thyself." Socrates emphasized that knowing yourself is the most important ingredient necessary in creating a fulfilled life. Even with these words of wisdom repeated over and over again, mankind continues to run amuck, experiencing lives of confusion. How can we know ourselves? What tools can we use to decipher the code of our chaotic lives?

We have heard it said many times, "We are the captain of our own ship, masters of our own fate." We have been told we are in control of the wheel, steering the course to our goals. As captains, we are supposed to be instantly ready to move with the wind to reach our planned destination. Yet, as we look around us, it appears that we are not the captains we would like to be. In fact, sometimes we seem to be out of control. We often feel directionless in the midst of a stormy sea.

The I, who thinks he or she is in control as captain of the ship, can change his or her attitude and behavior within seconds. An angry word, an accident, any number of events or experiences may trigger a change within us and suddenly the captain is different. Who is this new captain taking control of our lives? There seems to be a battle on board the ship, deep inside, tearing apart our minds and hearts.

Yes, we are captains of our own ships. And the way I see it, these are pirate ships. Each of our crews are made up of the many sub-personalities living within us. And the crew is planning mutiny.

The purpose of this book is to help you stop the battle, the war raging within you. It is a battle between your crew members who often have very different desires, preferences, goals and aspirations. The battle is causing too much pain and confusion. It is time to identify the different crew members who are represented as various parts of your personality. What is the purpose and desire of each crew member? What is each one doing for you? By learning more about your many sub-personalities, you can chart a course which satisfies all parts-of-you.

This particular process of discovering who you are is called the Infusion Integration Technique, which provides a tool for identifying, uniting and integrating all parts-of-you. It gives you an opportunity to integrate the individual units of thought that have significance in your life today.

To speak of a variety of parts-of-you is to imply that each of us has multiple sub-personalities. As we look closely at the concept of having not one but a multitude of different personalities within us, it is possible to conceive that these different parts-of-us could each develop their own special agenda, their own specific ways of thinking and behaving. Each personality could have its own desires and fears.

Our inner life could truly resemble a pirate ship.

LIVING ON A PIRATE SHIP

Imagine for a moment you are on an old-fashioned, square-rigged, sailing ship. You boarded the ship in the Bahamas, starting out on a pleasure cruise for a wonderful quest and exploration of the Caribbean islands. As your adventure begins to unfold, you notice that different crew members seem to be taking the position of captain each day. The new captain changes course and creates great confusion and consternation among the other crew members.

You begin to realize that this ship is made up of a motley crew of men and women who have left the world of laws and regulations. They are pirates in every sense of the word. Fighting the outer world has become a habit, for that is where they see their problems. All they know is conflict. They are in the midst of battle for control on board ship as they fight over food and space to sleep. The pirates constantly argue over which direction they should be headed, what port to enter, what treasure-laden ship to attack or with what other pirate ships to join forces.

The captain is always the strongest pirate at the time, the loudest, the most able to beat the others into submission. Once in a while, one of the crew will take over the bridge and become captain for a day, a month, sometimes for the remainder of the voyage; but usually there is another member of the crew, or a group, who will plan a mutiny and pull the captain down. The new captain will take over and set his or her own course on the seven seas.

On board there are always those who climb the mast and search for land. There is the ship's cook who rarely leaves the kitchen. A cabin boy does the bidding of everyone on board, since he's usually a stowaway. And, of course, there's the crazy one who causes so much commotion and confusion that he is put in chains down in the hold and never sees the light of day. If the crazy one escaped, who knows what he might do or what direction he might wish to go?

You are that ship, carrying a crew of personalities within you, each with their own agenda and reason for wanting to plan a mutiny. You are the passenger and crew members and in many ways confused and in conflict. The various parts-of-you, these aspects of yourself, often have different viewpoints and their own beliefs about reality.

At various times in your life—as a neglected infant, during an accident, a major problem at school, a divorce, or a death—a part-of-you will often make an important decision and/or adopt a powerful belief based on the information available at the time. The information upon which we make these decisions or choices is usually very limited, because we have usually not been trained to look for creative solutions to our problems.

When we are in the midst of turmoil, we often spontaneously, and almost subconsciously, make decisions, speak declarations, and adopt beliefs which may not be in our best interest. Sometimes a part-of-us, a sub-personality, adopts the position of becoming the keeper of a decision or choice. A particular part-of-us holds this belief for the entire crew, making certain our actions, behavior and experiences in life reflect that particular decision or choice. Other parts-of-us may believe differently, and want to behave in a way that would change our lives for the better, but the keeper of the decision will do everything in his or her power to hold his or her position until he or she is given a good reason to change it. The Infusion Integration Technique helps to provide an opportunity to change outmoded beliefs and develop creative solutions.

By looking closely at our behavior and experiences, we begin to understand our actions and behavior. At the age of forty-seven, I realized a part-of-me had made a lasting and profound decision not to become married. My love relationship of twenty years had ended. I had felt as if I were married during the relationship, but I wasn't. I had been very independent in my thinking and actions and marriage had rarely been discussed. Living together seemed to make more sense than the commitment of marriage. I observed that other women seemed to move into marriage easily and were sometimes engaged within just a few dates after the beginning of a romance. The fact that other women got married easily was interesting to me, since no one had ever proposed to me, not even as a joke.

Finally, while working with the Infusion Integration Technique, I decided to ask myself why I had stayed unmarried all those years. I asked the part-of-me who had made the decision to stay single what she was doing for me.

She said, "I am making certain that no man will take care of you."

Suddenly, I remembered a decision and an oath I had made at the age of thirteen when my father left my family. I had made a declaration which affected my life for thirty-four years.

When my father left I made a decision and stated to myself, "No man will ever take care of me!" By making that statement, I meant that I would become very independent and would not need to depend upon a man. My rationale was: if my father, who appeared to love me very much, would leave me, then no man could be trusted not to leave. So guess what? No man took care of me for the next thirty-some years. No man ever asked me to marry him. A very effective oath!

In the process of doing the Infusion Integration Technique, which is outlined in detail in Chapter 12, I was able to say, with some effort, "A man can take care of me." (It took great effort to be able to say, "a m-m-man c-c-can t-t-take c-c-care of m-m-me," without laughing or stuttering.) I was able to change the statement based on new information: a man could take care of me, and I could still feel free and independent, and not be fearful he would leave me. Approximately eighteen months later, I met my husband, who asked me to marry him two weeks after we met. With no prompting or knowledge of this story, he said the magic words to me: "I want to take care of you."

In countless examples over the past twenty-five years, I have seen the ways in which the Infusion Integration Technique can help change the inner landscape of the mind. As a result of the integration, which takes place internally, actions and behavior patterns begin to change externally. Within a short period of time, the outer reality of life reflects those changes.

Imagine yourself back on the pirate ship. You will find various members of the crew, parts-of-you, may be holding outdated decisions, choices and beliefs about men, women, work, study, luck, health, wealth—everything in your life. At the same time, other parts-of-you may disagree with those decisions or beliefs completely.

You've gone to school. You've read self-help books and attended workshops to change your life. Yet parts-of-you never participated. Some of the crew members were hiding away, holding onto a belief for dear life and making certain your experiences reflected that particular decision or belief. A part-of-you made the decision at age four, twelve, fifteen or twenty-two and that part still thinks he or she is doing something for you by his or her actions. The beliefs of each sub-personality serve to color your thoughts and feelings in all that you do.

What if the crazy crew member being held in chains down in the bottom of the ship were to get out? What if that persona became captain of your ship? What if he or she were to take command of your life? You'd probably find yourself headed in a totally new direction. Would you suddenly leave your job and take a credit card tour of the world? Might you move to the mountains or the seashore? Would he or she turn you into a drifter without aim or desire? Who knows. Are you really aware what the various parts-of-you want? Probably not. Most people have never taken the time to discover the fullness of who they really are.

This pirate ship, which is composed of you (whomever that is) and your crew members, is unique. It is important to note that no part-of-you can be forced to walk the plank. None of your sub-personalities can be sent to plunge deep into Davey Jones' Locker. You cannot force any crew members off the ship. You may attempt to lock away a part-of-yourself below decks, but you cannot avoid the screams and objections you will incur. You may continue the battle between the various characters within you, constantly tearing yourself apart, or you can learn to live in harmony with all of your sub-personalities as you sail the uncharted waters of your life.

CHAPTER 2

Peace on
the Pirate Ship

A new tonality is created
by learning the notes,
hearing, seeing, feeling,
being the sound of each tone.

I f you were to create a feeling of peace and an atmosphere of consensus on the pirate ship, your own ship of state, you would need to become acquainted with each of your crew members. Until you know the crew and are able to communicate and come to an agreement with them, setting your course will be more a matter of random luck than fulfilling your true desires.

You would be wise to take the time to find out about your crew's likes and dislikes, their favorite port of destination, what they enjoy doing. What are they trying to do for the ship and themselves by their erratic behavior? Why do they want to mutiny? What are the potential benefits to them for their own personal agenda? By interviewing and working with the crew members, you may have an opportunity to work out the differences between them and find a way to satisfy everyone on board.

The same is true inside of you. Lurking within the darkness and depth of your personality are parts-of-you who have certain beliefs and ideas that may not have been updated since you were a child, teenager or young adult. A wide variety of beliefs and behavior patterns are developed throughout our lives, and rarely do we stop to evaluate whether these beliefs and behaviors are serving us currently. Normally, we just react to each situation based on well-tried patterns which were effective in the past. We rarely make the effort to change our opinions or beliefs. We don't even acknowledge they are affecting us. Yet our sub-personalities with outdated beliefs may be keeping us from our goals, creating disease in our bodies, stopping us from having a loving, long-lasting personal relationship or interrupting the even flow of our lives.

The Infusion Integration Technique is a powerful tool that can change your inner atmosphere from a battleground to a sea of tranquility. Changing your inner landscape and reshaping the inter-action between all parts-of-you simultaneously changes your life. At the same time, the battles on the outer landscape also stop. In an almost miraculous way, you are no longer fighting the world. The people and events of your life change to reflect your inner experience. As you reconcile the differences and problems inside you, it is no longer necessary to create differences and problems outside of you.

The Infusion Integration Technique helps you to see clearly how this pirate ship of characters inside is mirrored to you by all the people around you. Every person in your life can represent a different part-of-you. Your family, friends, adversaries, co-workers and acquaintances play the roles and speak the words of the sub-personalities within you. They act out the different parts-of-your-being for you, often in an extreme way.

Each person with whom you interact can unconsciously play a role for you. Someone in your life may show you perfectionism or sloppiness, which you share, but they may show it to you at an extreme. An associate or family member may portray disgust or depression, silliness or seriousness, strength or rigidity. They may be showing you parts-of-yourself, for you have within you aspects of many extremes, expressed or unexpressed.

It seems you often bring into your life the various characters that you need to help you to see, experience and feel your thought patterns and beliefs. The people in your life, whom you know and meet each day and throughout the year, may represent sub-personalities within you. These sub-personalities (crew members) are struggling for recognition. They want to be heard and understood. When you do not listen or pay attention to sub-personalities who have long been ignored, then other people may be required to play the role of those personalities for you to see and hear.

The people who play these roles for you, whether it's your mother or father, a sibling, a boss or co-worker, whomever it is, often act out your inner submerged thoughts and feelings to an extreme. These people in your life may overact their parts. They say things which drive you crazy. They annoy you in so many ways. Their purpose is to show you your subtle subconscious traits.

Life is a type of "biofeedback system," an energy exchange of information helping you to see what you are thinking and feeling. The people and events in your life are acted out in living color in front of you, enabling you to recognize the beliefs you are holding. The way you see the people in your life and feel the experiences that you enjoy or detest is the result of the projection of your thoughts, desires, beliefs and fears. These thoughts and beliefs are shown on the big screen of your life, allowing you to understand and realize your inner self through projecting your thoughts onto the world around you.

Often you may try to change the people around you by arguing, cajoling or pleading with them. What if there were another way to change your experience of the world and the people around you? What if you could simply have a conversation with the part-of-you that each person in your life represents? What if you could create an inner landscape of peace, and your outer world, including all the people and events, began to reflect your inner peace? Infusion may help you to integrate the various parts-of-you, bringing about changes in your perception of life.

In the following chapter, we begin the process of getting to know you, all parts-of-you, by looking closely at the qualities, talents or possible roles of your sub-personalities.

CHAPTER 3

Changing Your
Inner Landscape

You have to be there to get there.
You have to be there always, to get there for sure.
Where do you want to go? Who do you want to be?

Let us assume, for the sake of argument, that you have within you a vast collection of different personae, parts-of-you who are being expressed at various times of the day, week or year. The persona is a personality—the way you act, look, dress, behave, talk, move, breathe, your posture, how you think and what you say. Your primary persona or personality is, or can be at any given time, distinctly different, depending on who you are with and what you are doing.

Let's say you have a unique general persona for family gatherings and a specific persona for each member of the family when you meet with them separately. Different personalities are visible in your work environment, one for your boss and another for your co-workers. You may change your persona again for social gatherings and for each person you meet, whether they be people you're attracted to or those you quickly want to avoid.

You have a persona for hiking in the mountains or sailing on the ocean, riding an elevator or flying in an airplane. The variety and richness of these various persona portrayals simply demonstrate the multi-faceted aspects of your sub-personalities. A specific persona comes forward to present its strengths and weaknesses for family, friends and co-workers, making you appear as an amazingly different person, depending upon what mood or sub-personality is in control at the time.

When a specific sub-personality becomes your persona, at that given moment it may make you appear as a different individual. Each sub-personality is able to characterize its interaction with other people in a unique way. Your voice, facial expressions, liveliness or retreating behavior combined with your viewpoint and opinions will reflect major belief systems held by that sub-personality.

These belief systems define the world of each sub-personality. Your major belief systems are an assemblage of decisions you make as a result of events that occur and your reaction to them. Often, decisions are made with limited information. (For example, as a child and young adult, you do not have access to all the information available on a given subject.) The subconscious sifts through limited data in the mind and makes decisions without considering a wider view. A decision-point marks the beginning of a core belief about life.

Each sub-personality builds his or her identity with patterns of beliefs. A sub-personality's (crew member's) strength depends upon the intensity of his or her beliefs and how much power and influence he or she is able to wield over the total being (all the members of the crew). Is she strong enough to sway all parts-of-you to her way of thinking? Is he powerful enough to become captain and make decisions for the entire crew? Whether a crew member is fully in control or not, he or she has the ability to affect activities and events. He or she attempts to get attention by trying to prove his or her point of view.

All of these different faces you show to the world are often important and necessary. Some of your activities require a formal presentation. Other events may allow you to be very casual in your manner and dress. When your interaction with people and events is effective and rewarding, then the sub-personality who is in charge at the time is being appropriate and effective. But when your actions and participation in activities bring you confusion and upsetting responses, then perhaps it is appropriate to examine what the members of your crew are trying to accomplish and why.

WHAT ARE YOUR QUALITIES AND TALENTS?

In order to define and get to know your inner crew (your sub-personalities), it is helpful to understand your personality patterns and feelings. The best way to begin is by thinking about your overall qualities and talents, not just who you are right now, but also who you would like to be or have imagined yourself to be.

I suggest that you dedicate a three-ring binder and note paper to use as you read this book. It is helpful to take notes and save the information you are learning about yourself. List your qualities and talents, your preferences, the descriptions of your sub-personalities, and the new scenario of your life.

Begin by listing your qualities. Realize that you probably have many extremes within you: you may be private and personable, neat and sloppy, dynamic and lazy. It is valuable to write these qualities on a sheet of paper, and list as many as you possibly can. A list of qualities and talents which I used follows. You may adopt those I have listed, whichever seem appropriate, and subtract or add your own.

QUALITIES

Caring	Loving	Sensual
Curious	Funny	Artistic
Creative	Playful	Musical
Efficient	Private	Diligent
Exciting	Serious	Spiritual
Energetic	Friendly	Dynamic
Confident	Intelligent	Romantic
Self-reliant	Optimistic	Reclusive
Enthusiastic	Nurturing	Powerful
Spontaneous	Interesting	Passionate
Adventurous	Discerning	Meditative
Communicative	Flamboyant	Responsive

Next take a look at your talents and possible roles. Roles refer to activities and careers you may have been interested in pursuing. You may have never been involved in these areas, but at one time you may have had some interest. Here is my list of talents and possible roles.

TALENTS AND POSSIBLE ROLES

Doctor	Cook	Pilot
Lawyer	Actor	Parent
Investor	Artist	Student
Designer	Writer	Teacher
Publisher	Sailor	Traveler
Politician	Sculptor	Scientist
Psychologist	Gardener	Researcher
Communicator	Promoter	Movie Producer
Business Person	Photographer	Environmentalist
Importer/Exporter	Philanthropist	Sports Enthusiast

Now take the time to describe your own qualities, talents and possible roles. This exercise helps give you an idea about some of the possible crew members on board and how to work with these sub-personalities as we proceed to describe our desires and goals.

CHAPTER 4

Uniting the Crew—
What Do They Want?

You may not get what you want
when you want it,
but it will be on time.

After you have described your qualities, talents and possible roles, it is important to discover what type of lifestyle you prefer. If all your sub-personalities were in balance, what would you prefer to have in your life? How would you describe the life of your dreams? As you proceed through the book, you will learn to evaluate your overall goals and desires in a way which will satisfy the majority of your crew members' needs and wants.

Your desires are tools through which you grow. You stretch and realize more of your potential as you move toward greater prosperity, abundance and fulfillment of your wants and needs. When you are excited and motivated, you are experiencing a sense of aliveness and an inner awareness of unlimited opportunities. Writing about your preferences helps to put a structure around your excitement to move you toward your goals.

The four major areas of our lives, the four cornerstones of the building of each life, are health, wealth, love and self-expression. At the central core, in the center of the building, is self-integration. All of your crew members will basically agree that these four cornerstones and self-integration are important to their lives and vitality. You could compare these cornerstones and the core to the actual masts, the keel and the structure of the sailing ship, the vessel itself. Each member of the crew will agree that they need the ship, even though they may want to take the ship in different directions. It is likely you will discover opposing goals and ideas that are in conflict.

THE CREW AGREES
TO PROTECT THE SHIP

Even though each crew member could describe different criteria for the four cornerstones of life and self-integration, as a first step, it is important to write about these elements in a general way, so your sub-personalities can be in agreement about the overall picture of your life.

As you begin the process of describing the four cornerstones of your life, pay attention to expressing how you want to feel, what you want to have and own, and write it as if it were already happening that way. To give you examples, I have described what I mean by the four cornerstones, self-integration and the basic preferences I wrote to create my new life.

FOUR CORNERSTONES OF LIFE
AND THE CENTRAL CORE

HEALTH: I feel extremely healthy and fit. My muscles are strong. I have no extra fat on my body and can easily maintain my perfect weight. I am thinking clearly and am alert and vibrant. My skin, hair and internal organs are perfectly healthy. I am in total balance and harmony all day, every day. I have an overflow of energy and awaken in the morning ready to greet the day happily and energetically.

WEALTH: I am receiving an abundance of money for my personal use. I feel freedom and excitement about what I am doing each day and feel fulfilled in my work and my life. Money comes easily, and I feel my prosperity, growth and development personally and professionally. I am wealthy and successful. My savings accounts are over-flowing as I invest in dynamic new enterprises.

LOVE: I love and am loved by the people in my life. I am in a loving, supportive, enjoyable relationship with a wonderful mate. I feel totally and completely loved in a non-co-dependent way, which means that there are no control issues. I am not controlling him and he is not controlling me. I feel safe and secure and complete in my passionate, beautiful, loving sexual life. We love to look at and touch each other. We give to each other abundantly and both receive completely.

SELF-EXPRESSION: I am creating and expressing my passion for life each day. I write, paint, sculpt, sing, dance, laugh, and play with delight. My life is a potpourri of joy as I open to my creative powers. My life is full of creativity, and I feel the excitement of the energy of all of creation working through me. I have the ability to understand other places, times and events and to be a major contributor to the health and well-being of the earth.

SELF-INTEGRATION: Each day I feel the power of expressing my deepest self in all my activities. I am integrated totally with my higher self and feel the energy and vitality of expressing my purpose and destiny in the here and now. All my separate personalities are now integrated into a beautiful, dynamic whole.

Take the time to write your own definition for health, wealth, love, self-expression and self-integration. If you like the way I have described these areas, take the time to copy these descriptions in your own handwriting and add whatever feelings or concepts which may come to mind. Always write in the present tense as if these ideas were already true in your life, whether they are or not.

THE CREW WANTS CERTAIN BASICS

Within each crew member or sub-personality, there are basic needs which are required to create a feeling of happiness. By focusing upon these needs and desires, the various parts-of-you can combine their energy to create what you want. Your environment and lifestyle can become fulfilling in every way.

When we described health, wealth, love, self-expression and self-integration, we wrote the descriptions in a general, unified form. In the following exercise, we continue the process by writing a general description of your preferred home, travel, play, feeling of independence, personal growth, and spiritual development in the present tense.

HOME: I live in a fabulously beautiful home, which echoes all of my favorite colors and designs. It fulfills my sense of style and taste and goes beyond my wildest dreams in terms of beauty, harmony, peace, joy and hospitality.

TRAVEL: I travel to wonderfully exciting, exotic places and enjoy every moment of the sights, sounds, smells, and feelings of delight. I am a grand explorer, moving about in style, ease and grace. I enjoy the thrill of discovering new places and wonderful people who welcome me with love.

PLAY: I play with gusto. I swim, sail, dance, play on the beach, walk through the flowers, sit and relax, meditate and feel the playfulness of life bubble up through me all day, in every way.

INDEPENDENCE: I make my own decisions easily and quickly. I follow my intuition, and use the power of greater awareness to make my life easy and comfortable. I am stable, financially secure and feeling great freedom in my wealth and abundance.

PERSONAL GROWTH: I am growing in wisdom, love, knowledge, personal understanding and in relationship to others every day.

SPIRITUAL GROWTH: I am becoming attuned to my Higher Self and open to greater awareness, so that I may be a clear vehicle for the love and wisdom of God.

WHAT DO YOU VALUE?

A very important aspect of your life to consider is values. What do you find valuable in your life? Your values are the base from which all your decisions are made. The order of priority in which you list your values can make the difference in how you decide what is important in your life. I encourage you to go through the process of writing lists, studying their implications and rewriting them.

For instance, in my first listing of values, I realized that freedom and achievement were high up on the list. When I put health and vitality at the top of the list, it made me realize what a low priority exercise and rest had been for me. I would often push myself far beyond my physical capabilities due to my need to achieve. Notice I replaced freedom with peace of mind and moved health, fun and happiness higher on my second list. With this change of order, I can make decisions in favor of fun, happiness and relaxation rather than considering achievement to be above all else. It is very interesting to see how you feel as you change the order of the lists. Your list may change over time. The two lists I have made are:

VALUES

LIST 1	LIST 2
Learning/Growing	Health and Vitality
Intelligence	Love/Compassion
Achievement	Peace of Mind
Freedom	Gratefulness
Love/Compassion	Intelligence
Creativity	Honesty
Health and Vitality	Learning/Growing
Gratefulness	Fun and Happiness
Contribution	Contribution
Honesty	Creativity
Passion	Intimacy
Intimacy	Passion
Fun and Happiness	Achievement
Peace of Mind	Freedom
Investing	Investing

HOW DO YOU ACHIEVE YOUR VALUES?

Having taken a look at what you value in life, it is equally important to know what your criteria is for having succeeded in each area. I was surprised to realize I did not have a criteria for success. Achievement was high on my first list, yet I did not feel as if I had achieved very much, even though I have had many successful events which should have given me a feeling of success.

I realized that having succeeded in the business world, having used my creativity in writing, having created a beautiful home, having found wonderful friends, having experienced abundance and having traveled around the world is by far enough achievement to let me feel successful in that area. You do not have to expect huge achievements in order to feel successful. Why not be happy if you pass a test, fulfill requirements for a job or have a wonderful evening with friends? Your criteria can be at any level you wish.

With no criteria or measurements for your values, it is as if you are floating on a windless ocean with no purpose or understanding of where you are going or why. How will you know when you are healthy? Do you need to be a certain weight, eat the right foods and stick to a stringent exercise program? Or is your criteria based more on what you can accomplish, how many hours you can work or play, or how much energy you have available to you?

What about your criteria for feeling loved? Must love always come from people outside of you, or is it possible that you can feel love inside of yourself? A friend of mine said there's only one person you are going to be with for all of eternity, and that is yourself. Why not fall in love with you and treat yourself as your own best friend? Perhaps your criteria for love and compassion can be generated inside your own mind and when it is reflected to you by others, you can simply rejoice in the abundance of love available.

Think about the criteria for each of your values, and be certain to allow room to succeed in each area.

CHAPTER 5

Gathering the Crew
for a Possible Coalition

It is only with the heart that one can see rightly;
what is essential is invisible to the eye.

Antoine de Saint-Exupery
The Little Prince

I n February 1990, I lost nearly everything: all of my money, my
boyfriend of twenty years, my health (I had a broken foot, rib and
cracked spine), and my business. I began to describe the various parts-
of-me. I learned what they wanted, and also discovered how angry
many of them were about the decisions I had made. They were upset
because I hadn't listened to my inner guidance and intuition. I had
blindly moved forward, letting my ego lead me into destruction.

What had happened to this person who had been working so
diligently to perfect her life? In September 1989, I became enthralled
with the idea of helping produce a movie about a real life drama
which had taken place in England in 1979. I read the book about "The
Green Stone" and felt that a movie about this story would be worth
making. In October, I flew to England with my two co-producers. We
met with the people who had found the Green Stone, and I purchased
the rights to the story. For six weeks, we traveled to the sacred sites
throughout the British Isles where the drama had unfolded.

In England, I was a guest of Robert Bolt and Sarah Miles in their
sixteenth century manor house. They offered to help write the screen-

play for the movie. Mr. Bolt had written some of the all time great movie scripts, including *Lawrence of Arabia, Dr. Zhivago, Ghandi, The Bridge on the River Kwai* and *The Mission*. I was scheduled to meet with big name academy award winning actors and actresses to star in the film. It was all very exciting.

I returned home in mid-November and learned that the investors who had promised to put in seed capital had backed out. In January, my inner guidance (intuition) was telling me, several times a day, "Take your money and run."

One more time I argued, "I'm doing fine. The movie will come together. The investors will arrive. There's nothing to worry about."

Learning from my experiences, I suggest when your intuition or a gut feeling is telling you that you're going in the wrong direction, pay attention. Get to the root of what you are feeling. Don't just try to override the message as if it is nothing.

Speaking of nothing, that's what happened throughout January. I was trying to maintain myself, my two co-producers and the expenses of two investment coordinators on the little remaining money I had saved from my years as vice president of two high technology firms.

On February 9, 1990, I went to a movie to observe an actress I was considering for the film. My mother went with me. There were steps inside the theater. After going up about ten steps, I turned to see that my mother was having difficulty climbing. I decided to go back down to help her. As I put out my foot, the movie went into a night scene and the theater became dark. I fell forward, landing on my stomach with my feet twisted up behind me. Mother came to my side as I struggled to get to my feet. I hobbled to a seat and watched the movie with ice on my foot. When it was time to leave, I could not put weight on the foot, so I hopped to the car. I went for an x-ray and learned that I had a broken left foot and broken right rib. Two weeks later, I fell off my crutches and cracked my spine. My doctor said with fire in his eyes, "You are not to do anything, or I'll put you in the hospital." I was bedridden for four months.

It has been said that all of us, at some time in our lives, must meet the Hermit. Some of us go to the meeting with dignity, and others go kicking and screaming. I went kicking and screaming. It all seemed so rude, to be stopped dead, unable to move. At the same time, the people I had been working with on the movie project also seemed to be stopped. Nothing was happening on the investment front. No money was coming in. I was still supporting the project. My savings were disappearing. I was in a panic.

I had always been the type of person, if something was bothering me, I could go for a walk around the block, change my energy from negative to positive, come up with a solution and feel much better at the end of my stroll. After my fall, I was unable to move and was forced to face my issues head on. I could not change the scenery. I had to look at my co-dependency, come to terms with my very strong and stubborn ego, and face my intense need to control my life.

I began to write about my pain and frustration, my sadness and loss. It was the "dark night of my soul." Yet now I am thankful for this experience. The change in me was profound. A larger explanation of the various elements of my personality began to unfold, leading me to the discovery of my sub-personalities. I learned about the various parts-of-me, what they wanted, and how we could work together. I do hope you won't wait for a dramatic incident in your life before you take the time to learn more about yourself.

As I was healing, during the months of April and May, a phrase a teacher of mine had quoted from the Bible began repeating over and over in my mind: "Seek ye first the Kingdom of Heaven, and all else shall be added unto you. And the Kingdom of Heaven is within you."

"What does that mean exactly?" I asked.

"It means just what it says," my intuition answered. "Raise your level of consciousness. Seek spiritual enlightenment, and all else— your material, emotional and mental desires—will be fulfilled."

So I studied many books to open my mind to thoughts of spiritual fulfillment. I prayed for wisdom and meditated to receive guidance and to clear my mind of the worries of everyday life.

In June, my money was gone. I sold most of my furniture, put things in storage, and moved into a tiny bedroom in my mother's small house. It was quite a change from my independent life to go home again. Yet I was grateful at that moment for a place to stay and to continue healing until I could go to work again.

A few days after arriving at my mother's house, a friend called and invited me to her lovely home in Palm Springs. She said she would pick me up on Saturday. I was delighted. A few minutes later, she called back and suggested that I come to her home at the beach

Friday night. She was having people over whom she would like me to meet. We would drive together to the desert on Saturday.

"Great," I replied.

When I got off the phone, I felt a tightness in my stomach, and my intuition seemed to be telling me not to go to her home at the beach. "Why not?" I asked myself.

The reply was, "You are too vulnerable at this time. It is best for you not to go meet those people on Friday night."

"That's ridiculous!" I thought. "I'm fine and I want to go."

One more time the stubborn, ego-based part-of-me refused to listen. I started to pack a suitcase. As I rushed around the corner of the small bedroom, I hit my right foot on a chair and broke my fourth toe. It was unbelievably painful. I cried the rest of the day. My mother could not console me. I thought this meant another six weeks of lying in bed.

(As my intuition had suggested before I broke my toe, I did not go to my friend's house. A few weeks later, I learned that a man who was dying of cancer had been at my friend's home at the beach that Friday evening. It had been a very emotional experience for the people who attended. In many ways I can see that my vulnerability and desire to help may have been too much for me at that time.)

A week later, I was surprised to find that I was able to hobble around with my broken toe. I met with friends I had not seen for several years. They invited me to a church service in Santa Monica at the Agape Church. They said that the African-American minister, Reverend Michael Beckwith, was quite remarkable. The church was alive with the joyful energy of a mixture of people of nearly every race and many nationalities who sang together and danced in the aisles. I decided to go with my friends the following Sunday. It seemed that any positive experience at that point could be helpful.

We arrived early at the church, and I walked down the hallway to the meeting room. Suddenly, someone opened a door, slamming it into my broken toe. I dissolved into tears. (My soul has a way of getting my attention.) I hopped the rest of the way to the main room to a seat near the front, off to one side, with my right foot up on a chair.

The room was softly lit and lovely music floated over me as the pain subsided, and I sat quietly in meditation. A picture began to form in my mind. I saw myself being carried on a litter down a road. (It seemed best not to walk, not even in my meditation.) On my right I saw a beautiful crystal city glistening in the sun. On my left was a burned-out city, covered in smoke, with people warming their hands over fires in garbage cans. The message I heard in my mind was, "Do not deviate from your path. Keep moving toward spiritual fulfillment."

The meditation ended, and the room exploded in music and song as the Reverend Beckwith came on stage. After the singing, the Reverend stood at the middle of the stage, not behind the pulpit, and began to talk. It was Father's Day, and the name of his sermon was "Father of Lights." Listening to that sermon was the culmination of all that had happened to me during the previous six months in the "dark night of my soul." He spoke about our service to God and Christ, and that our job is to "shine." We are to give out our light and love to everyone we meet. I sobbed as he spoke. The message went deeper and deeper into my heart until I had an overwhelming sense of my need to surrender to God, to the universal power that is in all things. I wanted to fall down on my knees and bow to the love that had been trying to help me all my life. In my stubbornness I had resisted this love, and in doing so, I had caused myself so much pain.

Finally, I could hold back no longer. I was sitting off to the side of the audience, next to the wall, so I didn't think I would make a spectacle of myself. I moved off my chair and onto my knees. I bent over in the aisle and placed my head in my hands on the floor. Tears poured forth from the depth of my soul. I asked for God to forgive me for not listening. So many times I had not listened to His guiding voice. I had made decisions that I knew were not in my best interest out of stubbornness to have my own way. Feeling unworthy, I asked that I might have the opportunity to serve Him.

I felt the warmth of love and forgiveness flowing through me, and the feeling of being full beyond measure was almost too much to endure. The pain of knowing I had been such a fool, mixed with the power of knowing that God's forgiveness is infinite, seemed to be breaking the shell of my ego. My heart seemed to be bursting apart, my mind was splitting into little pieces.

Each time Rev. Beckwith paused, I would think, "Now I can quit crying and return to my chair." Then he would offer another phrase which would strike as lightening in my soul. At one point he said he didn't know where these words were coming from. He hadn't planned his sermon this way. He apologetically stated, "This was supposed to be a sermon about Father's Day, wasn't it?" The images he was painting with his sermon were breaking apart the remaining resistance I had within me. As the shell around me broke, I was becoming completely available to God's love, which seemed to be all around me, within me and overflowing to all those around me.

He finished his sermon, and I began to dry my eyes. I felt weak and waited a few minutes before picking myself up off the floor. Then an incredibly beautiful male voice began to sing the song, "You Are the Wind Beneath My Wings." I dissolved again into tears, my head resting on the floor.

When that song was finished, a chorus of voices filled the room with, "I release, and I let go. I let the spirit run my life. I am free in the spirit. I am only here for God." The congregation joined in the singing, and as they rose from their seats, people came forward to pull me to my feet. They held me in their arms and comforted me. They truly understood, and they were with me.

From that time forward, I decided that my personal commitment was to allow God to work through me, to be a vessel for love, peace and light. In the days following my experience at the Agape Church, I floated in the peaceful emptiness beyond thought. I let go of my desires and opened my heart to Christ and God.

A month later, in July, I was well enough to walk without limping and started working again. My background had been in marketing and advertising. I was thinking about how I should proceed when a picture came into my mind of a man that I had met a few months before who owned a public relations agency. I called him and he said that his company had no positions open. But he did suggest I call the fund-raising director at the local unit of the American Cancer Society. I called immediately and went in for an interview that afternoon. They hired me as a marketing consultant for two months. After working there ten days, the Marketing Director of the unit left for another job, and I was given that position. The office was just eight blocks from my mother's house where I was staying to recuperate from my injuries.

As the months passed, I lived very simply, saving my money and becoming balanced internally and externally. I found that my mind and heart were letting go of the outrageous demands I had placed upon myself throughout my life. I had written the descriptions of my various sub-personalities, and I listened to their requests and tried to harmonize and fulfill them.

In February 1991, I was given an extravagant four bedroom, three bath, beautifully decorated home with a swimming pool and jacuzzi, high on a hill with a marvelous view of the distant mountains, to house-sit for just $700 per month. I had this huge palace all to myself. It was pure luxury. In April, I was given a $2,500 trip to Bali. I went as a speaker (for just one hour of work in a two-week journey). I refer to these events as gifts, because the opportunity to house-sit and pay so little for rent and the trip to Bali came with very little effort. During this time, I was meeting new friends and was feeling better physically.

On July 7, 1991, I was feeling wonderful about life. I felt supported by God and the universe. The clearing of my old thoughts had been helpful, yet there seemed to be a few things which would be nice additions to my life, such as: a meaningful relationship, a permanent home of my own, abundance, a truly healthy body and the ability to leave the nine-to-five world of jobs so that I might write and travel. I thought it would be interesting to talk to the different parts-of-me once again. This time, I would really investigate and clarify my preferences.

I spent the July 4th weekend alone in the big house with a view of the mountains. On July 7, I wrote: "I have been swimming in the pool and lying in the sun. I am rather tan for the first time since I was a teenager. The weather has been magnificent, and I sit now in my comfortable office in this lovely house looking out the window at the beautiful, fluffy, white clouds in the blue, blue sky.

"I meditated in the garden today and the birds sang to me. I walked on the beach and saw the waves crashing to shore. For the first time in many years, I feel truly relaxed. It is such a joy to surrender my body, mind and emotions into God's love. I feel at ease and at peace internally and externally."

It seemed appropriate to listen very honestly to all parts-of-me, to let them express themselves in such a way that my own mind would be settled into creating what they wanted, needed and desired. If all my sub-personalities could rally together, perhaps the demands of my crew could move into a harmonious pattern. Maybe they could agree on a course of action and quit pulling me apart. Maybe we in the crew could look together at our similarities rather than our differences. If we could come together as one being, opening our hearts and minds to higher consciousness (Christ consciousness), to the kingdom of heaven, then perhaps my life could become an even more successful pattern of existence.

In order to establish clarity, I decided my sub-personalities needed to describe what we prefer and what we don't prefer. Then we could turn the process of creation over to the seemingly magical properties of the universe (the God force). When we quit fighting internally, that force of creation can easily work through our lives so "all else will be added unto you."

On July 7, 1991, I realized so much had changed in just one year. I had worked with all parts-of-me and had used the Infusion Integration Technique to pull myself together.

One year earlier, in July 1990, I would never have guessed that I could be living high on a hill, in a beautiful home, in luxury. In July 1990, I had lost nearly everything (or so I thought) and had moved into the small bedroom at my mother's house and was recuperating from my injuries. I did not have the job at the Cancer Society. I did not have a clue what I would be doing next. The feeling of going to Bali was just starting to percolate in my mind.

To begin the process of clarification, I decided to write down what I liked about my current life.

- I enjoy this beautiful house with the wonderful view.
- I treasure the quiet and privacy.
- I love being able to write on this Mac computer.
- I love my art and the accessories I have collected.
- I respect and honor my talents and abilities.
- I love to pray and meditate twice a day.
- I enjoy the wonderful feeling of peace and tranquility.
- I like the feeling of abundance.
- I love sleeping soundly and awakening refreshed at dawn.
- I love not being rushed around from place to place.
- I like the feeling of relaxation.
- I like feeling good about myself.
- I like having everything efficiently organized.
- I love being healthy, attractive, athletic and able to move easily.
- I love having so many wonderful friends to share my life.

Take the time to write what you enjoy about your current life. What are the positive aspects about your life at this moment?

I then wrote some additional ideas of things I would like to add to my current life. (Notice how these topics are also written as if they were already happening in my life.)

- I love owning my own home.
- I love owning a beautiful car that serves me well.
- I love having money to purchase what I want.
- I love my fabulous husband, who adores me, and I adore him.
- I love traveling to foreign countries.
- I love meeting many wonderful new friends.
- I love being my perfect weight, enjoying strength and stamina.
- I love feeling young, enthusiastic and excited about life.

Write your list of what you love, like, enjoy. Become enthusiastic and fill in as many marvelous ideas as you can.

I then decided to write a continuous paragraph about what I don't prefer. I just let my mind flow as I thought of the things I don't enjoy: humidity, bugs that bite and annoy me; people who are rude and stupid, angry and easily upset; long plane flights in crowded seats; subways; small, dark rooms; boring nine-to-five jobs; inconvenience; injustice; ugly art; discordant music; sickness; accidents; poverty; loneliness (but I do enjoy being alone); depression; sadness; sad death and dying scenarios; cruelty in any way; people being treated badly; useless activity just to be busy; confusion and noise; unpleasant, dirty, ugly environments.

Write your list of what you do not prefer in your life.

I then wrote about what I have always wanted to do or would enjoy: I love writing; sculpting; meditating; massage; swimming; dancing; playing; singing; speaking to groups; the ballet; concerts; lovely hotels/resorts; beautiful homes; quiet, peaceful surroundings; time alone; delicious food; beautiful flower arrangements and gardens; delightful fragrances; gorgeous vistas; loving friends; photography;

relaxing music; dramatic and humorous films; horses; intelligent and exciting men and women; fine art; elegant china; beautiful linens; comfortable furniture; fashionable clothes; being an author of best-selling books.

Write about the things you have always wanted to do or would enjoy. Remember, you are listing preferences. Aim for the sky!

What would I do if I could do anything I wanted for a year? I would travel around the world with the man I love, to places that intrigue me and write and take photos of my travels. I would go with introductions to each place I visit. I would be welcomed and shown the intimate, personal aspects of each location: the beautiful out-of-the-way gardens and restaurants, the charming avenues, the lovely attractions and the people that bring a place to life.

List what you would you do if you could do anything for a year.

What do I consider to be my life goals?

- Living in a beautiful home with a great view, filled with special treasures I've collected from around the world.
- Enjoying a wonderful and loving, intimate relationship.
- Having more than enough money for my needs and desires.
- Traveling to interesting places.
- Feeling healthy in mind, body and spirit at all times.
- Exciting, intelligent, spiritually aware friends.
- Feeling love for and from all the people I know.
- Helping to create peace, health and prosperity for all people.

Now write your life goals.

CHAPTER 6

The New Scenario
of Your Life

Intense desires are often creative desires.
Powerful, impelling goals that come true
have the full force of the self, emerging from bondage.
We can literally see, smell, taste and touch success.

W hat does it mean to assume the role of captain of your ship? What is your role as the decision-maker? You must decide what kind of life you want to create. What is the new scenario of your life? You have an opportunity to weave the outrageous ideas and discarded dreams that you hold with you and take a daring leap. If you care to try, you can change your life completely.

The new scenario of your life can be just as real, just as viable, just as concrete as the one you are currently living. The difference is that your current days are a reflection of the memory patterns of many years and experiences you have lived through in the past. You have used the images and experiences shown to you by family and friends to create your current environment.

If at any time in your life you have been able to make a leap in consciousness, to do something you thought impossible or to experience an event that seemed as if it were a miracle, then how easy it should be to manifest a life which is fulfilling in every way. Even if you haven't had proof that changing your mind changes your reality, then you can simply make a new decision about what pleases you. It's called going over the top, allowing yourself to move into a new realm of experience.

Do you know what this requires? You need to adopt a new way of thinking, acting and being. This is nothing short of a revolution in consciousness.

A NEW SCENARIO

My life is my finest expression of creativity.

I once heard it said that we are the stars in our own movie. We are the writers, producers, directors, casting agents, fashion designers and stars of our own show. Unfortunately, many of us do not seem to recognize our starring role. We act like bit players in our own movie. We sometimes feel like the spear carriers in a cast of thousands, standing in the hot sun in a Cecil B. DeMille movie.

What would happen if you decided to become the star, the leading lady or leading man, in your own movie? Would you act differently? Would you speak different lines in your dialogue with co-actors? Who would you be? What would the background sets look like? Where would you go on location?

As you may remember from my story in the preface of this book, I learned to make a list of items and events I preferred to have in my life and wrote the date by which they would happen. Over the years, I have suggested to many people that they should make a list of what they want. The results have been incredible.

One example that amazed me was the manifestation of a preference written by a lady who worked with me at the Lodge at Pebble Beach. She had heard me talking about making a list of what I wanted and setting a date for it to happen. She wrote that she wanted to own the house of her dreams by a date just three months in the future. I was surprised she had written such a preference because she and her husband had five children and not much money. They owned a small house in a modest neighborhood, and the idea of being able to leap into the house of her dreams seemed rather extravagant. I did not want to put a damper on her dream, nor did I want her to become financially strapped, so I suggested she add to her preference: she would own the house of her dreams that she could afford.

She did not discuss the idea of a new home with her husband. She just put her list in her dresser drawer. About a week later, her husband came home from work and said, "I'm getting tired of this neighborhood. Let's look for a new house this weekend." Of course, she agreed.

On the weekend, they explored the Monterey Peninsula, and decided to drive up into the hills overlooking the Carmel Mission and the beautiful views of Carmel Bay. They saw a new home sitting out on a point of land with incredible views. A man was working in the garden in front of the house. There was a for sale sign posted. They stopped to ask him about the house. He was the owner and builder. He was having financial problems and needed to sell.

The house had three floors. The living area was the second floor and upstairs there were three bedrooms. The bottom floor was unfinished. The builder suggested that he could create three additional bedrooms for the children downstairs. He volunteered to carry the mortgage with a low down payment and a balloon payment in five years. They were able to buy the house of their dreams and were moved in and settled in less than the three months she had written on her list. A year later, her husband was given a promotion and an increase in salary, which allowed them to save the money for the balloon payment.

As you can see, the way in which the list manifests can be unusual and intuitive. The events and coincidences can be remarkable as you watch your desires become reality.

Another example of the results of list-making was when my mother, Elaine, bought her first Mercedes-Benz automobile. For years she had been saying that she would like to own a Mercedes. Family and friends made it quite clear to her this car was beyond her budget. In June 1979, she once again stated her preference. "I want a Mercedes." By now this statement had become humorous.

"If that's what you want, Mother," I said, "put it down on paper. Write it down and say I will be able to afford a Mercedes-Benz by. . . What date do you want it?"

"By my birthday in August," she replied. She wrote her request on a piece of paper and put it in her purse.

"Be sure to add which you can afford," I said.

On her birthday, she and my brother were driving by a Mercedes dealership. She asked him to stop so she could look at the cars. A few minutes before they arrived, a man had driven into the dealership needing to sell his used Mercedes. Mother was introduced to the man, and she bought the eight-year-old Mercedes in excellent condition for five thousand dollars. She only needed to give him a down payment, which she received from the sale of her car. He carried the paper, and she paid monthly payments, which she could afford.

Preferences can be rather extravagant and outrageous. And sometimes drawing a picture or finding a photo of what you desire can help to clarify what you are visualizing. One man I knew was an artist. He was always complaining because he didn't have a decent studio in which to do his artwork. I suggested he write a description of the studio he wanted and specify the date by which he would like it to become available for him.

"I'll do better than that!" he exclaimed. "I'll draw a picture." On a scrap of paper he drew a sketch of an English Tudor mansion with a circular drive and a round tower by the front door.

"Oh, really!" I said. "Have you lost your mind? Are you moving to England? I thought you just wanted a studio."

"This is the picture which came to my mind," he said. "We'll see if your list idea works."

I thought for certain this time the list would fail. Surely, he'd gone too far. A few days later, a friend of his called him on the phone and asked if he'd be interested in managing an estate in Pebble Beach. The owner, who is a famous entertainer, was away most of the year, and my artist friend would have full run of the house. He went for an interview and got the job.

You guessed it! The house was an English Tudor mansion with a circular drive and a round tower by the front door. There was a huge basement that he was able to use for his studio, and he enjoyed the opportunity to receive a salary while he painted and lived in luxury.

Moving from obscurity to fame can be an interesting transition. A team of two interior designers with their office in a small town on the San Francisco Peninsula made the decision to become internationally famous. When I met them, they didn't even have pictures of the homes they had decorated. I suggested that they write their preferences for the expansion of their business on paper. They agreed to try the list and wrote: "We will be internationally famous designers. Our projects will appear in major interior design magazines. We will be designing projects around the world in one year's time."

About two weeks after writing their preferences, a friend of theirs contacted them and asked if they would be interested in traveling to China, all expenses paid, as guests of the Chinese Consul on International Trade. They would be consulting with the Chinese government and trade representatives about designing furniture for the U.S. market. With great excitement, they said yes.

While traveling in China, they were able to buy wonderful artifacts, antiques and silk fabrics. They began to include these very beautiful items in their interior design projects. They presented seminars and lectures to other designers in the San Francisco Bay area, showing slides of their beautiful blending of contemporary and oriental design. They hired a professional photographer and entered design contests. They won the national *Interior Design* magazine contest and were flown to New York to receive their award. Their project, in full color, was given primary placement in the magazine. Pictures and stories of a variety of their projects appeared in all the major interior design magazines, including *Architectural Digest* (a premier interior design magazine).

Before the year was over, they were receiving phone calls to do design projects in Hong Kong, Venezuela, Paris and London. They were internationally famous in less than one year's time.

Using your mind's ability to create events that may advance you in your profession can be very helpful. One friend of mine, Robert, was taking courses for his Masters Degree in Psychology. He was working and carrying twenty-eight units at one time (a very heavy load), including statistics, which was a difficult subject for him.

In the midst of his concern about the upcoming finals, I suggested that he write: "I will receive all A's on my report card this semester." He resisted, telling me that I had lost all touch with reality.

"Why not just write that you will receive all A's?" I asked. "What have you got to lose? Just put the words on paper."

Finally, he wrote the statement while shaking his head.

Robert took his finals and was very nervous. When the report card came in the mail, all A's were staring at him. He thought there was some mistake. He went to meet with the professor who taught statistics, and asked if he had meant to give him an A. The professor did reveal that many of Robert's mathematical solutions were not correct, but he could see that Robert understood the logic involved. And Robert's essay on statistical analysis was brilliant. So the professor felt compelled to give Robert an A, since he seemed to understand the purpose of statistics and its applications better than anyone in the class.

The reason for A's in the other classes were all somewhat similar. Robert hadn't completed the tests perfectly, but in the eyes of each teacher he deserved an A for a variety of unusual reasons. Of course, he had not tried to receive A's with no effort, but Robert was delighted and in awe of this seemingly magical process.

In business, it is usually the job of the Sales Manager to set goals of gross sales for the company in the following quarter. A few years ago, I sat in on a sales meeting of the Container Division of the International Paper Company. The Sales Manager was leading his sales people in goal setting. He put a number of several hundred thousands of dollars on the blackboard. The sales people all agreed this goal was achievable.

I spoke up and said, "Since you all agree on this sales goal, why don't you go ahead and double it?"

There was a large cry from the audience, "No way!" they called out nearly in unison. "We can't do that! Too much!"

"Why not just write the number on the board?" I asked the Sales Manager. "What can it hurt to see a bigger number in front of you? You don't have to commit to that number, but maybe it could happen."

The Sales Manager looked at me. He seemed to understand my purpose and wrote the larger number on the board.

Everyone in the audience stared and shook their heads.

"Now double the number again," I said quietly.

A rumble rose through the room as people moved in their seats as if they were getting ready to leave. "She's crazy," I heard mumbled from around the room.

The Sales Manager paused for a moment and then wrote the doubled number on the board. "It's called stretching your imagination," I said. The meeting was adjourned.

Three months later, I received a call from the Sales Manager. In a very excited voice he exclaimed, "It happened! We did it!"

"What did you do?" I asked, having forgotten for a moment about the events at the sales meeting.

"There were a series of strange events. New customers came to us requesting to buy our products. Regular customers ordered two and three times their normal number of containers. We hit the sales number we had written on the board, which was four times greater than our plan for the quarter. The sales people put out extra effort. It happened! It's amazing! I wouldn't have thought it was possible."

If I were to tell you a hundred stories, it would not be as important as your first manifestation from the writing of your list. The idea of this material is for you to use and discover the power of your own magic.

When observing how making a list works, it appears the writing of the dream, desire, or idea on paper seems to take the concept from the nebulous realm of thought into the material dimension, bringing it closer to reality. It is similar to the process of building a house. You may conceive the layout of the home in your mind, but when you commit the design to paper, it becomes more real. If you create a model of the building, as some architects do, the reality of the project becomes easier to imagine. Therefore, placing your requests on paper allows you to begin to manifest what you are imagining. You may develop more insight into your desires or preferences as you evaluate what you truly want.

It is important to remember that you are creating a feeling as you think about the items, the events and the people you might desire to be part of your life. That feeling can be yours right now, this moment. Yes, the feeling is in your imagination, but the end result of life's experiences is your internal feeling of joy, happiness and pleasure. Creating events or material things cannot create the feeling, they can only add to your own personal happiness. The things, events and people can be the icing on your cake. The cake is to care about yourself and your life. The icing is just for fun.

The idea of writing a list of your preferences or requests to God or the universe is similar to doing physical exercise. As you allow yourself to imagine what you might prefer in your life, you are stretching your mind and imagination.

If you can remain neutral and unemotional about your preferences and do not feel you must have these things to be happy, you won't block manifesting in unexpected ways. You will be able to enjoy what comes to you, rather than becoming attached to a particular manifestation. Your neutrality releases fear, allowing the infinite creativity of God to supply your needs and desires.

As you read the chapters which follow, you will discover when you do not receive the abundance, the relationships or the health you desire, it is often the result of a part-of-you blocking these experiences. One of your crew members may be stopping your dreams from happening because they believe they are doing something for you. So it is worthwhile to make your list, or the new scenario of your life, as I and many others have done; but it is equally important to learn about yourself and your beliefs which may be stopping you. You need to begin by accepting yourself and your life as it is right now! It may not be perfect, but events and experiences have happened for some reason. You can learn to feel happy within yourself, even if you don't have the things, people or events you prefer.

On July 8, 1991, I decided to stretch my mind and imagination, and write a new script, a new scenario of my life. I wrote my scenario in the present tense, as if it were already happening. I imagined the experiences I would like to live, and I let myself pretend I was living the scenes in this yet-to-be-released movie, this new life.

As you read my dream scenario, think about your own ideas of adventure and excitement. Open your mind and heart to the possibility of living life to its fullest, feeling free, aware, alive, happy and experiencing your ultimate joy. Be extravagant!

THE NEW SCENARIO OF MY LIFE

Written July 1991 to manifest by July 1992

I feel absolutely wonderful! I am excited about life and living it fully and abundantly. I am totally overjoyed with all aspects of my environment, my health, my wealth, my love life and relationships, my creative expression and my spiritual fulfillment.

My body is strong, flexible, slender, and healthy. I have stamina, and each day my senses seem clearer. I weigh my perfect body weight, and my muscles are toned. My skin glows with health, and my eyes sparkle with delight. My hair is shiny and strong. I look, act and feel youthful. People tell me I'm radiant, and they think I am younger than my years. I have the energy to accomplish my activities and never seem to be tired, yet I rest easily and well.

I have a lovely place to call home in the country with a beautiful, expansive view. It is large enough to have weekend guests and delightful parties. It is decorated with artifacts I have collected from around the world. My closet is full of comfortable and elegant clothes.

My husband is the love of my life. We are compatible on every level. He is young, handsome and successful. He is devoted to me and my happiness. He showers me with love, praise, presents and understanding. I love him with all my heart and soul. He is my ideal personified, and he has given me a new meaning to life. He makes me feel adored, treasured and honored. I feel more of a woman, more special than I have ever felt before.

Most of my time is spent with my husband, traveling to beautiful places, spending time alone, relaxing, enjoying tranquility and peace. He understands and practices meditation and prayer with me. He is very evolved and aware. He feels and expresses that I am both an asset and a joy to him.

I have many wonderful friends who are very supportive. I spend happy hours writing books and poetry. I appear on television, speak on the radio and before groups.

I have wonderful children in my life who are sweet, loving, friendly and creative. I have delightful pets that are always fun, entertaining and loving.

I will now absorb, reflect and meditate upon this scenario. I will prepare to live in the divine essence of pure being, manifesting in the here and now the most excellent events of my life.

SEE IT, FEEL IT, BE IT,
SENSE THE SOURCE,
EXPECT MAGICAL FULFILLMENT

- See what you prefer in your mind's eye.
  Describe in detail what you want to manifest as if you were in its presence. What are the colors, the textures and the design of the objects you want to own or the details of the event you want to experience? Write the description of the person you would like to meet.
- Feel what you have described.
  Let yourself experience the touch, taste, sound and emotions you feel as you imagine the object, the event or person.
- Be what you desire.
  Imagine actually becoming a home, a yacht, an event, a profession or the loved one you want to meet. Move your mind into the feeling of being what you have described.
- Sense the source out of which the experience is manifest.
  Imagine the energy of the pulsating force that creates all things and feel the source of the power of manifestation.
- Expect magical fulfillment.
  Create a feeling of expectation and develop an attitude of optimism as you follow your intuition. Expect unusual events and coincidences to help manifest your desires.

Now write the new scenario of your life. Be flamboyant! Have some fun with it. You can always change it later. You can make your scenario more conservative, but for a few minutes take the time to write what would be an outrageous script for your life so you can feel some of the adventure and excitement you have within you.

THE ROLE

To get an acting role, you must study for it.
You must know so much about the role
that you become it—heart, mind and soul.
All which is not the role must be discarded.

After having written the new scenario of my life, I decided to write an abbreviated description of the starring role—my role. This overview of the role would give me an opportunity to begin studying for the part. This was a very new and different role for me. Most of my adult life I had been a professional working woman, a marketing vice president and owner of my own businesses. I had never been married. I was a macho woman. This would be quite a change, and it would take some study and research to learn how to play this role.

MY NEW ROLE

I am the wife of a successful, fabulously wealthy, international businessman. I am his hostess, lover, friend, confidante and companion on trips to world capitals, meeting the rich and influential. I am dynamic, beautiful and talented with unlimited stamina. I write best-selling books, appear on television and speak on the radio and before groups to promote them. I appear to be about thirty-five years old and I'm slender, healthy, sophisticated, intelligent and can speak on many subjects. I arrange great parties and am a grand hostess. I invest in worthwhile enterprises and help to bring peace and harmony to the planet.

Now write a brief description of your new role.

Allow yourself to believe in your creative ability.
Just as a lump of clay can become a glorious statue,
your life can become fulfilled.

CHAPTER 7

Creating
a Wish Book

Ask and you shall receive.

The next step is to create a wish book, which is a collection of pictures cut out of magazines depicting some of the articles, events, and people you would like in your life. Find pictures of your preferences—places you'd like to visit, a car you'd like to own, a house that suits your fancy, furniture you prefer, art, jewelry and any other articles that make you smile when you look at them. Cut out phrases from the magazines that are appealing to you, such as: "Art is never an extravagance," or "Less effort, more style." Place the photos and phrases in plastic covers that fit in your three-ring notebook. You can browse through your picture book, and add, subtract or change your preferences. This entire process should be fun, not serious. This is a visual opportunity to once again clarify your preferences.

I made a marvelous wish book. I found gorgeous fashions, pictures of Bali and destinations in France. I even cut out a picture of men whom I thought were very attractive. One had a wonderful smile and looked at ease. Another was watching as his wife showed him all the things she had bought while out shopping; he had a great look of agreement and happiness that she had found what she wanted. A third man looked tall, blond and very elegant. The caption said "To the Manner Born." This one gave me the impression of a true gentleman, elegant and at ease with wealth. The similarity between these pictures and my husband, Tom, whom I met three months later is quite amazing. Tom has an easy smile and completely enjoys and encourages me to shop for what I want. He's tall, blond and has similar facial features to the gentleman in the picture. And he is a perfect gentleman.

Remember, you are defining preferences. You are not trying to create these images and events. You are to relax into the idea that these would be what you would prefer in your life. Yet you do not necessarily know the desires of your heart. The full experience of love, laughter, peace and harmony to create a joyful life for you may be more expansive and perhaps quite different from what you describe. The wish book and the writing of your new scenario give you a starting point to know who you would like to be and what you desire, right now. These are not demands that you must have in order to be happy.

It is important to turn the creation of this new scenario over to your Higher Self, to God, All That Is, the Universal Force, Christ (whatever name you wish to use) and allow your intuition to guide you as the clues for your new life begin to unfold before you.

For example, I had thought when I wrote the new scenario of my life, that I wanted to live in Europe and be married to a European man. After I wrote the scenario and received the agreement of the different parts-of-me, I turned the creation of my new life over to God. I said, "These are my preferences. Please provide me with something similar to what I have written or better." In this pronouncement, I released all the preferences and desires I had listed. From that time, I focused on enjoying each moment of the day as much as possible.

The Energy of Creation provided as good, if not better, a scenario for me. As of this writing, in June 1994, I am living with my beloved husband (we were married October 3, 1993) in a beautiful home on an eight-acre estate overlooking a one-hundred-eighty-degree view of a gorgeous pine valley nestled under majestic mountain peaks. The village, one-half mile away, looks European, yet it is in the mountains of California. Tom looks European, but he was born in Southern California. We share a similar background. We grew up watching the *Mouseketeers* and *Leave It to Beaver*. As children we were raised in the same religion, and our love of gardening, helping in the healing profession, traveling, decorating, food, etc., are almost identical. Also,

Tom, being a successful physician, along with his entrepreneurial pursuits, is able to provide many elements of the extravagant lifestyle I described in my new scenario.

I left the door open for the universe to provide the most ideal new life for me. It takes some patience and a lot of trust; most importantly, you must develop the ability to relax and live life in this moment, even though everything in your life may not be ideal now. Relaxing into the flow of life, as it is, without judgment or condemnation, helps you to become a magnet for the preferences you hold and the desires of your heart.

You do not need to hate your current life in order to change it. You created the life you are living now for particular reasons, and to learn certain lessons. Acknowledge and congratulate yourself on your creativity, whether what you have created is a comedy, tragedy, romance or deadly dull. You can change your life if you want to, utilizing patience and a deep understanding of the members of your crew. I had to work at clearing, updating and integrating many parts-of-me in order to allow for the beauty and harmony that I am now experiencing. In the chapters that follow, you will learn about the Infusion Integration Technique to help you master the process that will allow you to receive the abundance you desire.

THE TIME ELEMENT

So how long did it take for me to manifest the new scenario of my life? I first started writing the descriptions of the different parts-of-me in June 1990. At that time, I started my wish book and cut out some pictures of fashion, places I would like to visit, etc. During the following year, I got a new job at the American Cancer Society, moved to the lovely home with a pool that I described earlier and expanded my network of friends. I had not dated and was beginning to believe that I might be an old maid, since my only companion for dinner and the movies was my mother. She's lovely, but I had the desire to have a wonderful man in my life.

On July 4, 1991, I decided to get serious, and I wrote the new scenario of my life. I added pictures of wedding gowns and the man I had described. In truth, I had never thought much about being married, since I had declared my oath, so successfully, that "no man will take care of me." It was January 1990, when I reversed that decision and stutteringly stated: "A m-m-man c-c-can t-t-take c-c-care of me !"

I met Tom October 5, 1991, just three months after writing my new scenario. He was the central core of manifestation of that scenario, and our living together is better than I could have imagined. As I first began to consider my preferences, wrote the new scenario and defined the various parts-of-me, I went into a period of deep introspection. I began to examine closely what beliefs and concepts were blocking me from living the desires of my heart and holding me in old patterns that no longer worked for me.

And thus my inner work began.
There are other parts-of-me, other sub-personalities,
who often do not agree.
They think they're doing something for me
as they try to stop my progress
toward what they think is the wrong direction.

In the chapters that follow, you will find descriptions and examples of the Infusion Integration Technique. You will learn how to understand and utilize the energy and strength of all parts-of-you—the entire crew. You will, especially, learn how to work with those parts-of-you who may be marching to a different drummer. These wayward crew members think they are doing something for you, while they arrange for strange and upsetting events to stop you from living your planned scenario—the new script you would like to live. You must know as much as possible about you and clear away all your inner obstacles in order for your life to unfold in a new way.

CHAPTER 8

Intuition

Intuition senses the directions to go in for most benefit,
it is self-preserving, has a grasp
of underlying motive and intention,
it chooses what will cause the least amount
of fragmenting in the psyche.
          Clarissa Pinkola Estes, Ph.D.
          Women Who Run With the Wolves

E ach person has a magnificent tool, which has often been forgotten in our culture. It is rarely discussed and is not usually
included in our educational process. This tool is called intuition or
inner knowing. It provides the opportunity to know and feel what is
best for you at all times and in all places. It has often been called
women's intuition and men's gut reactions, but the process is the same
for both men and women. The process is listening to inner guidance,
which helps you know if you're on the right track.

I have often been asked, "How can I know when I am being guided
by intuition, or when it is my ego or past programming which is
telling me what to do?" In order to receive the clearest intuitive
answers to your questions, it is helpful to quiet your mind and relax
into a peaceful feeling.

After you have posed the question, the first answer that you sense
or hear in your mind is often your intuitive guidance. The argument
that follows is quite frequently your sub-personalities trying to add
their input. The most reliable aspect of intuition is to pay attention to

how you are feeling in response to the question. Intuition may generate a feeling of knowing beyond words, or it may take the form of an idea expressed in words. Intuitive guidance has an edge of freshness and excitement to it. It doesn't feel like your normal patterns of thinking. It doesn't seem to be coming from your logic or memory.

You may have heard people say, "I knew I shouldn't have done it. My intuition told me to be careful," or "I had a gut feeling that I should stop and pull over. Because I stopped, I avoided an accident (a problem, some confusion—whatever)."

In the chapters that follow, you will be learning about the various crew members that inhabit your ship. Using the Infusion Integration Technique, you will learn to converse with parts-of-you who may hold beliefs, concepts and ideas that are preventing you from experiencing the desires of your heart.

During all of these conversations, integrations and development of a consensus, you must learn to listen to your intuition so that your life may run more smoothly. You must pay attention to your feelings and allow yourself to be led by your gut reaction.

Your intuition can be developed by paying attention to how you feel. So many of us have learned to disregard our feelings because it didn't seem safe to express our sadness or joy. We had to keep a stiff upper lip and not let anyone know how we were reacting to events or statements directed at us. I am not saying we need to let ourselves fall apart or act crazy with happiness. I am saying that our intuitive knowingness can mean the difference between success or failure, between happiness or depression and, sometimes, even life or death.

In the chapters that follow, you will read about sending a part-of-you, a member of the crew, to the creative part-of-you to come up with three solutions for whatever problem you are trying to solve. It will be stated that you do not need to consciously know what those three solutions are at the time.

What is the creative part-of-you? It is that aspect of your consciousness that is unlimited. You have within you immense creativity. You are able to access millions of thoughts that are available from the greatest computer ever designed, your human mind, to make your decisions. You are involved in the creativity of the universe.

Therefore, when you go to the creative part-of-you, you are contacting an infinite supply of creativity. You are asking for guidance at a much higher level than the limited conscious mind can give you. Your conscious mind can see, hear, feel, taste and touch what is in front of you now and can access your past experiences.

Your intuition is the part-of-you that delivers information from your entire being, including the creative part-of-you. Your intuition is able to give you the clues, the brainstorms, the bright ideas, the hunches that will direct you easily and quickly in a positive direction toward the desires of your heart.

You do not need to know how it happens. You don't need to know where that bright idea came from. The creative part-of-you, working in alignment with your intuition as a messenger, can, and will, help you to change your life.

From a scientific viewpoint, you can observe the mind as an incredible computer, which will give you back the information you feed into it. Over time, we have all been programmed with negativity, whether from our parents, teachers, co-workers, television or movies. Negative, fearful thoughts, ideas and concepts are not difficult to find in our culture. Yet within you is the ability to change the negative programming you have digested over the years. You can take charge of your life. You can learn who you are, what you are thinking consciously and what is going on in your subconscious by careful observation and asking the appropriate questions. Ask the questions, and the answers will come. It may seem that I am making this sound too easy. It can be easier than you might think.

In order to truly understand yourself, the trick is to ask questions that can be answered with more than a yes or no. And don't make throwaway statements, such as: "Well, I guess I'll never know the answer to that!" The answers are within you. Expect the answers to be there for you, and they will be. Ask clearly and without hesitation. Be ready to experience surprise and often a kind of "aha," as you realize that you knew the answer all the time, but hadn't recognized it.

Your inner knowing, your intuition, is truly awesome. You cannot learn how to use it at a university, but you can allow it to work for you. All you need to do is feed your intuition daily. How do you feed your intuition? By listening to it. By feeling it. By paying attention to it. By not disregarding it.

Why am I so adamant about listening? Because I have found that not only do we create our desires, we also manifest our fears. I nearly died because I didn't listen.

In August 1971, I was working at an advertising agency on Wilshire Boulevard near the Ambassador Hotel in Los Angeles. After work, I rode the elevator down to the parking garage, four floors under the building. I walked into the small room which led to the cars and passed a man dressed in a guard's uniform. I glanced into his eyes, and a voice in my head (a loud thought—my intuition) said "Run." I didn't listen. I started arguing with my intuition, "Why should I run? I'm tired. It's late. Why should I run?"

Before I could reach the door, the man grabbed me around my neck and thrust a knife up to my throat. My first thought was, "Oh, so that's why I should have run!"

He started pushing me across the room to the opposite door. I could barely breathe as he held my neck tightly. I tried to loosen his arm with one hand and said to him the all-time great statement, "Calm down, you're hurting me." (No one would believe that statement as dialogue in a murder mystery.) At that moment, the other elevator bell rang. My attacker transferred the knife from my throat to my back.

The elevator door opened and two men started to come toward us. He stabbed me in the back and ran away. The two men pulled me into the elevator as my lung collapsed. I slumped to the floor. I thought I was dying. The pain was unbelievable. They half-carried, half-dragged me to the guard's desk on the main floor to wait for an ambulance. Policemen passed in front of me asking questions. I stared at them and tried not to pass out. My continuous prayer was to ask God, "Please let me live. And if I do live, please make me an instrument of your peace."

Three weeks later, after my collapsed lung healed, I tried unsuccessfully to help the police find my assailant. The police chief said I was lucky. There had been five other stabbings in the Rampart Division on that day. I was the only one who survived. Needless to say that didn't make me feel much better.

I continued to try to work but it seemed that everyone I talked to told me stories about violence. I became an unwilling magnet for terrible stories. I lived in constant fear.

I stayed at my job until Washington's Birthday, February 22, 1972, when the police came into the advertising offices where I was working. They told everyone to vacate the building. There was a bomb threat on the fifteenth floor—our floor. That was the final straw. I decided to move out of Los Angeles and back home to Carmel where I could heal from the experience of living in overwhelming fear. It took three years of long walks on the beach and the help of a wonderful counselor to move myself from fear to anger to freedom. I was able to once again walk easily on the street.

Over time I pieced together the beliefs within me that may have caused this terrible incident. I remembered that during my teenage years I had felt a deep fear of being attacked. At night in Carmel, I stood on the beach with my back to the road, trying to build my courage. I didn't succeed in changing my fear. Finally, I manifested the attack in the parking garage at the age of twenty-seven.

This was my hardest lesson in learning to listen to my intuition. Yet after this event, on occasion, I still continued to be stubborn and obstinate. I often got into trouble by trusting my logic rather than my almost magical intuition. I had to learn the hard way by making mistakes, falling and losing almost everything (literally), before I decided that intuition was much more trustworthy than my logical training from the past. It certainly was more trustworthy than my ego, which always seemed to argue and create blockages along the way. I have found that logic, the process of how you design a plan or project, can be helpful in creating a course of action. But it is very important to listen to your intuition first, and check in with your intuitive guidance every step of the way.

Is intuition magical? It often seems to be other worldly in that your intuition can tell you something you may not know consciously. Yet the process of intuition may turn out to be just one of the many unsolved mysteries of our very complex and powerful minds. We do not yet understand the mechanism of intuition for we currently have a very limited understanding of the brain. Just because we do not understand the source of our intuition does not mean we should not use it. Many of us do not understand the complex design of our digestive systems, yet we continue to eat without concern.

CHAPTER 9

Twelve Ways
We Interact
with Life

Life experience hones our ability
to see, feel, hear, taste and touch to the fullest.

Now that you have listed your qualities and talents or possible roles in this drama called life, you can begin to see that you are made up of a variety of concepts and beliefs. The number of possible experiences available to you grows in proportion to your understanding of how complex you really are.

Each of our lives reflects a process of interaction with other human beings and nature. Through that process of interaction, we grow and develop, utilizing each experience as a stepping-stone to future experiences.

In order to understand which part-of-you, which crew member, is reacting to current experiences, it is helpful to identify and define your major sub-personalities or crew members. I have divided these interactions with life into twelve primary areas or categories. These categories are meant to help you see the wide variety of possible personalities within you. There can be more than one representative in each category which can be a mixture of both male and female parts within us.

These twelve major sub-personalities with their variety of opinions are available to serve as your personal board of directors who can meet with you at your inner conference table and help make decisions about your life. The twelve represent specific areas of interest, and thus you can determine how to create an unlimited and fulfilling interaction with life without neglecting any of your important talents and interests.

There are obviously more than twelve sub-personalities within each person, since I am defining a sub-personality as a part-of-us which is holding a particular belief. As you use the Infusion Integration Technique, you will be changing and modifying those random parts-of-you who are maintaining various concepts and beliefs which are keeping you from achieving your goals and receiving your heart's desires.

It is an interesting adventure to discover and describe twelve distinct and opinionated sub-personalities living within you. The twelve major sub-personalities can act as your profound primary advisors in making decisions about your values, your use of time and your goals and desires. By describing the sub-personality representing each area of life, you will develop a deeper awareness and appreciation of your complexity.

TWELVE MAJOR AREAS OF INTERACTION WITH LIFE

1. BASIC HUMAN NEEDS:
   RELATIONSHIPS, FOOD, CLOTHING, SHELTER
   This part concentrates on your intimate interactions with life: loving relationships, delightful food and surroundings.

2. EDUCATION
   This part is interested in learning, teaching, educational systems, and gathering information to make you more aware.

3. HEALTH AND HEALING
   This part represents the healing professions, medicine, exercise, nutrition, nurturing and caring about other people.

4. ENVIRONMENTAL PROTECTION
AND GOVERNMENTAL SYSTEMS
This part-of-you is interested in politics, social policies, justice,
saving the planet, animals and the future of mankind.

5. ARTS AND RECREATION
This part enjoys art, music, dance, drama, crafts, sports,
amusement parks, boating, flying, etc.

6. COMMUNICATIONS AND MEDIA
This part may be a writer or speaker and interested in the
news, documentaries, public relations and reporting.

7. SCIENCE AND TECHNOLOGY
This part enjoys science fiction shows, mechanics, computers,
studying the universe, gadgets and new inventions.

8. TRAVEL AND TRANSPORTATION
This part likes to travel, explore new places and may be
fascinated with cars, trains, airplanes and spacecraft.

9. BUSINESS AND TRADE
This is the business part-of-you who values money and
activities from which you receive money.

10. PARENTING THE NEXT GENERATION
This is the father/mother part-of-you who cares about children
and their welfare whether or not you are currently a parent.

11. LOVING THE CHILD WITHIN
This is your inner child who never grows up, but always likes
to play and have fun, discover new things and enjoy life.

12. SPIRITUAL DEVELOPMENT AND HUMAN POTENTIAL
This is the part-of-you seeking higher wisdom, greater
knowledge, and a connection with God and the universe.

Look carefully at these twelve major areas of interaction with life. Take a moment to allow yourself to imagine that living within you are sub-personalities representing each of these areas. You might think that you don't have a representative for each of these categories. You might feel you don't have a scientist or governmental systems type of character as a sub-personality within you, but I suggest that this exercise be treated like a game. Pretend you are writing about characters for a book or movie. What would be the characteristics of each of these sub-personalities if they were a part-of-you? It is fun to make up the characters and give them names, even if you're not certain that they truly exist within you.

Using your list of qualities, talents and possible roles, you can describe your sub-personalities in each of these twelve major areas and begin to understand the characteristics of these advisors among your crew members.

For example, using my list of qualities, talents and possible roles, I have described each of my sub-personalities in the twelve categories. I gave each of my crew members a separate name to help create their own identity. As I considered the different categories, it felt as if I were describing characters in a book or play. The process helped me to discover parts-of-myself I had not considered. I looked at facets of my personality which I had never before truly defined.

TWELVE MAJOR SUB-PERSONALITIES

1. *BASIC HUMAN NEEDS:*
RELATIONSHIPS, FOOD, CLOTHING, SHELTER
Simone, the Sensualist
Talents/Roles: Artist, cook, designer, gardener, psychologist
Qualities: Loving, friendly, passionate, sensual, enthusiastic

2. *EDUCATION*
Paula, the Publisher
Talents/Roles: Publicist, writer, networker, promoter, teacher
Qualities: Confident, efficient, dynamic, energetic, optimistic

3. *HEALTH AND HEALING*
Clara, the Healer
Talents/Roles: Counselor, psychologist, researcher, teacher
Qualities: Loving, nurturing, optimistic, confident

4. *ENVIRONMENTAL PROTECTION*
AND GOVERNMENTAL SYSTEMS
Darion, the Philanthropist
Talents/Roles: Environmentalist, politician, consultant
Qualities: Powerful, serious, confident, dynamic, discerning

5. *ARTS AND RECREATION* (I described three in this area.)
Ann, the Actress
Talents/Roles: Artist, communicator, student, teacher
Qualities: Dynamic, spontaneous, funny, confident, attractive

Verite, the Poet and Sculptor
Talents/Roles: Designer, painter, writer, creator
Qualities: Energetic, passionate, sensual, discerning, romantic

Morgan, the Martial Artist
Talents/Roles: Sports enthusiast, student, traveler
Qualities: Energetic, determined, playful, dynamic

6. *COMMUNICATIONS AND MEDIA*
Nancy, the Networker
Talents/Roles: Consultant, politician, communicator, writer
Qualities: Friendly, enthusiastic, energetic, curious, interesting

7. *SCIENCE AND TECHNOLOGY*
Alison, the Astronomer
Talents/Roles: Scientist, writer, student, researcher
Qualities: Curious, efficient, serious, intelligent

8. *TRAVEL AND TRANSPORTATION*
Laine, the Explorer
Talents/Roles: Photographer, sailor, pilot, importer/exporter
Qualities: Adventurous, confident, self-reliant

9. *BUSINESS AND TRADE*
Bryant, the Tycoon
Talents/Roles: Builder, investor, promoter, publisher, producer
Qualities: Dynamic, enthusiastic, confident, discerning, efficient

10. *PARENTING THE NEXT GENERATION*
Martha, the Mother
Talents/Roles: Parent, psychologist, healer, cook, teacher
Qualities: Loving, energetic, efficient, optimistic

11. *LOVING THE CHILD WITHIN*
Soleil of the Sun
Talents/Roles: Sports enthusiast, student, promoter, gardener
Qualities: Playful, funny, spontaneous, enthusiastic, creative

12. *SPIRITUAL DEVELOPMENT AND HUMAN POTENTIAL*
Helena of the High Country
Talents/Roles: Writer, philosopher, researcher
Qualities: Private, serious, efficient, reclusive, self-reliant

As you can see, I have discovered within me the possibility of these twelve plus sub-personalities, each with their own talents and qualities. By giving them a name of their own, I have created an identity that can now be addressed even more directly.

MALE AND FEMALE

You may notice that I used male and female names in describing my twelve sub-personalities. We each have male and female hormones working within our bodies. Interestingly, we all began our lives as little girls in the womb. The male hormones eventually change the physical body for nearly half of the children born, and, in those cases, a boy child emerges.

We have access to both female and male aspects of our being. These aspects are described as the yin and yang in Eastern cultures. The famous psychologist Carl Jung named them the anima and animus. Jung expanded his theory of these powerful forces making them underlying polarities found in the mythology of all cultures.

The female (yin/anima) aspect is defined as having the attributes of nurturing, caring, intuitive perception and receiving. The male (yang/animus) aspect has the attributes of action, assertiveness, analytical and logical thinking, projecting talents, ideas and giving.

We need both the male and female aspects to live a balanced and fruitful life. We achieve balance by both giving and receiving, by achieving in the world and by relaxing and enjoying the fruits of our labor.

If you decide to use names in describing your sub-personalities, do take a moment to reflect on the reasons behind choosing either the male or female aspect to define that part-of-you. I have finally discovered that I can be strong and effective in the world and still maintain my feminine self. It seems that men are gradually learning to be more sensitive and caring in the world and still maintain their masculine selves.

DESCRIBING THE CREW

As I look at each of my sub-personalities with their specific qualities and talents, it is possible to identify who they are. I can discover what their ideas and beliefs are about life. I can determine how they would like to dress, where they would like to go and what they would like to do.

The following exercise is similar to describing characters you might include in a novel or a movie script. The difference is that these characters live within you and often are in conflict with one another. It is important to remember that you may not be living these roles out in the world, but within you is the desire to act out these roles. (For instance, I am not currently living as an actress, but there is a part-of-me who would love to act.) These sub-personalities only indicate a certain set of patterns, which you are now investigating. Whether you live out the full potential of your sub-personalities is yet to be seen. Many of the desires of your sub-personalities may be fulfilled effectively when you include them in the completed scenario of your life.

In the descriptions of my inner characters you will note that there are extremes represented in their descriptions and their desires. You will see a widely varied cast of characters. You probably also have a cast of characters buried deeply (or not so deeply) within you. You, too, may have assembled a strange and unlikely crew living within you. By knowing who they are and what they want, we are taking the first step toward a harmonious integration of these very different personalities. As you read the following descriptions, begin to think how you will write about these categories and the amazing characters (crew members) living within you.

1. *BASIC HUMAN NEEDS:*
RELATIONSHIPS, FOOD, CLOTHING, SHELTER

Simone, the Sensualist—Artist, cook, designer, gardener, psychologist: Simone enjoys experiencing her five senses and notices the tiniest nuances of beauty in every aspect of her environment. She loves delicious food, fine perfumes, flowers and art. Simone is attractive to others because of her radiance and passion for life. A loving personal partnership brings her great happiness. She wears designer fashions made of sensuous fabrics in warm, inviting colors. She loves swimming in tropical waters, making love. and massages. She has a beautiful home filled with exotic art and furnishings from around the world. Wonderful friends bring her love and entertainment.

2. *EDUCATION*

Paula, the Publisher—Publicist, writer, networker, promoter, teacher: Paula is bright, efficient, conservative, yet has flair. She publishes books and publicizes people and events. She is interested in the news for the sake of education and influencing decision-makers. She is serious and maintains that newsmakers make the difference. She is interested in helping people regain the joy of learning through innovative, creative methods of education.

3. *HEALTH AND HEALING*

Clara, the Healer—Counselor, psychologist, researcher, teacher: She is plain, but attractive, simple in dress, quiet, humble and reserved. She helps other people as much as possible. She spends her time working with the seriously ill and counseling active people in their relationships and careers. She reads about the latest in healing techniques and hopes to help bridge the gap between alternative methods of healing and the current modalities of medical science.

4. *ENVIRONMENTAL PROTECTION AND GOVERNMENTAL SYSTEMS*

Darion, the Philanthropist—Environmentalist, politician, consultant:
Darion is always dressed conservatively and fits well in the upper echelons of society. He is able to express his opinions clearly and efficiently and works well among the corridors of power in New York and Washington. He has even thought of running for the Senate. Darion donates large sums of money toward projects to help the environment and to develop creative expression.

5. *ARTS AND RECREATION* (Three Representatives)

Ann, the Actress—Artist, communicator, student, teacher:
She is pretty, spontaneous, lively and excited about life. She exercises to look healthy and she wears extravagant, brightly colored clothes. She takes singing and dancing lessons and appears on television and in movies.

Verite, the Poet and Sculptor—Designer, painter, writer, creator:
Verite dresses in avant garde clothing and her house is almost all studio with a lot of light and plants everywhere. She is a free spirit who takes classes in painting and sculpting and writes poetry. She expresses herself creatively on canvas, paper, silk and in clay, bronze and stone. She loves drama, music, solitude and nature.

Morgan, the Martial Artist—Sports enthusiast, student, traveler:
Morgan loves practicing tai chi and yoga. He is physically fit and strong as he studies the techniques of movement while integrating and balancing his inner knowing with his outer form. He dresses simply and comfortably and is in harmony with all of life and nature.

6. *COMMUNICATIONS AND MEDIA*

Nancy, the Networker—Consultant, politician, communicator, writer:
She is flamboyant, exciting, full of life and always ready for another party, dance, ball or extravaganza. She loves opulent designer fashions and elegant interiors—all to provide a backdrop for gatherings of wonderful people. She is full of fun and wants to link people together and help them meet each other for whatever reasons. She enjoys hostessing exciting parties for influential people.

7. SCIENCE AND TECHNOLOGY
Alison, the Astronomer—Scientist, writer, student, researcher:
Alison is delighted to investigate the secrets of the universe, the ever-spinning galaxies and cosmic theories. She reads and digests scientific data and correlates it to life on this planet. She doesn't care about fashion or hair styles. She would spend her days in the observatory recording the latest quasars and mapping the Milky Way. She is fascinated with technological developments in all of the sciences.

8. TRAVEL AND TRANSPORTATION
Laine, the Explorer—Photographer, sailor, pilot, importer/exporter:
Laine dresses in khaki, safari-type clothes and hiking boots. He is casually groomed, confident and ready with one simple bag and camera to go to Bali, India, Tibet, Africa, Istanbul, Argentina, Brazil, the pyramids at the Yucatan and Egypt. He likes out-of-the-way places with strange sounding names. He enjoys traveling, stopping to explore the local culture, and then moving on to the next adventure.

9. BUSINESS AND TRADE
Bryant, the Tycoon—Builder, investor, promoter, publisher, producer:
Bryant is always dressed impeccably. He uses his intellect to consult with businesses and build a personal fortune, which will enable him to invest in building projects, resort properties, publishing and movie productions. He is a financial wizard and knows good investments.

10. PARENTING THE NEXT GENERATION
Martha, the Mother—Parent, psychologist, healer, cook, teacher:
Martha loves children and enjoys helping them to learn about life and creativity. She delights in their growth and development as they interact, utilize their senses and begin to communicate their own thoughts and ideas. She appreciates a child's imagination and how a child can create characters and stories from bits and pieces of what he or she has learned about life. Martha sees herself as a model for children and young adults, so she continues her own growth and development and nurtures herself as she takes care of others.

11. *LOVING THE CHILD WITHIN*
Soleil of the Sun—Sports enthusiast, student, promoter, gardener:
Soleil enjoys swimming, walking through the forest and on the beach,
watching movies with lots of popcorn, being silly and making people
laugh. She is spontaneous, enthusiastic, creative and as friendly as a
little puppy. She wears casual, comfortable clothes and ties her hair
back out of her face. She loves to be spoiled with fun presents and
wonderful surprises.

12. *SPIRITUAL DEVELOPMENT AND HUMAN POTENTIAL*
Helena of the High Country—Writer, philosopher, researcher:
Helena is wizened and strong of spirit. She prefers very simple clothes
and a rustic environment. She wants to read and write great books. She
wants to spend hours meditating and going for long walks in the
mountains and at the seashore. She would allow a few close friends an
occasional visit for a few hours, but prefers solitude.

You will note in number five, Arts and Recreation, that I have
listed three sub-personalities. That is because one part-of-me who
enjoys the arts would like to be a performer, and the other an artist
and poet, plus the sports enthusiast has his own style. They are three
distinctly different sub-personalities.

As you write the descriptions of your sub-personalities, allow
yourself to see the various avenues of life you have looked at, thought
and dreamed about. The purpose of this exercise is to learn more about
your various personas and their distinct characteristics. Take the time
and effort to truly describe each character's nature, desires, clothing,
environment and talents. This can be a wonderfully creative activity,
allowing you to expand the vision you hold of yourself.

Now identify each of your sub-personalities in the categories
mentioned. Discuss their talents and qualities, name them, and write a
brief description of each of them. Allow yourself to adopt their point
of view. As much as possible, imagine becoming that part-of-yourself,
as you describe your sub-personalities.

As you proceed in this book, you may discover you have more than twelve sub-personalities. You will meet various parts-of-you who may be causing problems or blocking your path. They do not need to fit into the twelve parts-of-you that are described in this chapter. This is meant to be a creative exercise to begin to identify your major, predominant sub-personalities with whom you can reach a consensus about your life's goals and purposes.

When you are working with the Infusion Integration Technique, you will be asking the parts-of-you who are causing the problems to tell you what they are doing for you. You might ask their age and/or for a description of that part-of-you, but it isn't altogether necessary. The important information will be what the parts-of-you believe they are doing for you by causing the blockage in your path, the discomfort, the problem, etc.

The next step is to create a circle to indicate how interrelated all these different parts-of-your-being truly are. The circle's circumference is the totality of your personality. The center of the circle, as the center of your being, is where each of the sub-personalities meet and begin to merge into the integrated potential of who you truly are.

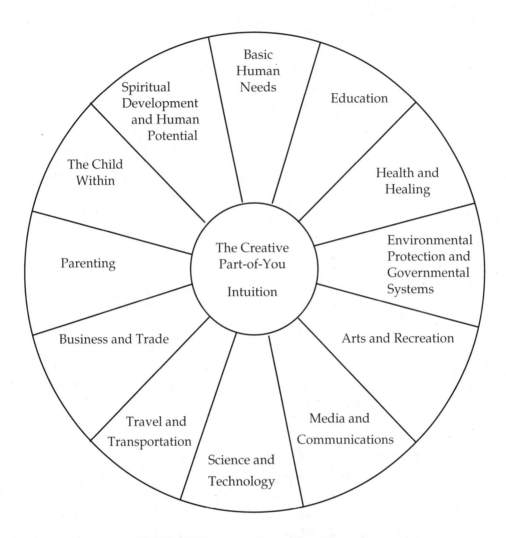

THE WHEEL OF TWELVE MAJOR SUB-PERSONALITIES

Here are your twelve major sub-personalities, the areas of interaction with life at a glance. You can put the names of each of your twelve primary crew members in the sections of the circle. The center circle represents the creative part-of-you, your intuitive self in touch with God and the universal flow.

THE TWELVE SUB-PERSONALITIES COMMENT ON MY NEW SCENARIO

I then asked my twelve major sub-personalities what they thought of my proposed new role and the new scenario of my life. (Remember, this was written in July 1991.) I asked each to add information from their own perspective.

1. *SIMONE, THE SENSUALIST:* We've been out of the social swirl for several years. I can't remember when we last made love. Can you imagine? How old did you say we are? Ninety? I mean, really. This is absurd. Not even a kiss, no handholding, not even the possibility of a date. Upset? Who me? At least in the described scenario there is a making love portion of the movie. I want to feel this life with my senses. The house helps. The beauty of it is wonderful, but we do need the missing ingredient—love, a man as companion, partner and lover. And getting married doesn't seem like a bad idea as long as he's young, sexy and full of life. I'm more than willing to do my part. Let's get out there where someone wonderful can see us. There are eight million people in the Los Angeles basin, and Verlaine hasn't been interested in any man in the three years she's been here. Really, I'm ready. You've got your bill of health (and the bills to prove it), so let's move it.

2. *PAULA, THE PUBLISHER:* Boy, have I been put out to pasture. Helena and Clara have really been running the show. I don't even get to read a news magazine anymore, let alone the newspaper. How am I to know what's going on? We hardly know what movies are playing. This new scenario seems to have some room for me to operate, but we need to get out of this pattern of accidents and pain. I can't operate well from this level of survival. Do you think maybe we could get out and get something done rather than just going to another doctor to see if we're well? If we're ever going to influence anybody, then we've got to get ourselves in shape and move into a wider arena. Let's make some news. Let's publish some books. Let's do something newsworthy. I'll work on it. We gotta have a hook.

3. *CLARA, THE HEALER:* Paula and Ann were always a little radical, but I do understand their position. I'm a little tired these days. It seems that the whole planet, and everyone on it, needs to be healed. All this giving of my time has been a bit difficult on the body. I guess if I'm supposed to play my role appropriately, I must heal the mind, body, emotions and spirit of the host body—my own body—first. Well, that is news isn't it? So all the emphasis on walking, eating correctly, living in balance is, first and foremost, the number one priority for Verlaine. I was a little disgruntled about us not getting ahead on the book, but now I understand that this exercise, this healing of Verlaine, is more important than trying to heal others. We can do the best job of healing personally, and then, by the way, others may be healed through the process of her living well. I say, let's go ahead and change the script. The new scenario makes sense to me.

4. *DARION, THE PHILANTHROPIST:* Well, I do understand the pitfalls of working through the system, and I do prefer not to be directly involved in the political process. I like the scenario—there is a possibility of meeting the right people and thus influencing change through the power elite. Positioning is very important and I do suggest you keep your eye on the target and not get dissuaded by possible interference from the more "flighty" members of the crew.

5. *ANN, THE ACTRESS:* I like what we're doing today, because I can play any role you set for me. For years I've been playing the little worker bee, the nine-to-fiver and the giver-to-all-who-would-take. I would enjoy this new role. Obviously, we will need cooperation from the crew to get out and exercise, slim down and study up on the life of the wealthy society people. I don't need to be on stage or in the movies to be satisfied but I do need a new challenge, a new role, because this old role has bored me to tears (especially the little business suits and the sitting in the office looking out the window). I need to be utilized. I've got a lot of talent waiting to be tapped. I make a great entrance, can read my lines perfectly, and can carry off the role of the wealthy, educated, talented woman, wife of the rich, famous, interesting guy who loves her. Why not? Let's get to it before I die of boredom.

VERITE, THE POET AND SCULPTOR: We could do something artistic! Why not set up a table in the office with some clay? We could sculpt just a few hours a week. Would it hurt? No. It would feel good. Can't you understand that it is imperative to your health that you take time to create with your hands, not just words on paper? Using your visual senses will be wondrous. Yes, I like the scenario as long as there is time for me, and you have to start making that time now! We will be happy with beginning a statue immediately. Solitude and nature are nice, and I want to create with my hands!

MORGAN, THE MARTIAL ARTIST: The best we have ever felt physically is when we were doing yoga and the short time that we studied tai chi. The scenario talks about being the perfect weight and having stamina, etc. It is imperative that we do physical activity to create the kind of health and activities that you are describing. There has been a distinct tendency to do nothing in terms of exercise. That must be changed. We are willing to work hard to help you have the strength and reserves you desire, but all the crew members must participate in taking the time to exercise, do yoga, tai chi, swim, dance, use the exercise bike, walk and run, now.

6. *NANCY, THE NETWORKER:* Well, I couldn't have done better myself. Actually, I did help write the new scenario. If we don't get moving, living, exuding enthusiasm, we will lose whatever little momentum we had going in this life. In other words: We'll die. Got it? As you know, life is people to me. What else is there? The landscape, the environments we move in are just backdrops for interaction with people. Yes, that's my business—public relations. We could be old and tottery and meditate the remainder of our lives away. At least your current meditation practices do give us some more energy to move, go and do. I'm waiting for the show to begin.

7. *ALISON, THE ASTRONOMER:* Where in your scenario do you acknowledge my interest in science and especially in the under-standing of the cosmos? I need to have my expertise and background in studying many different scientific pursuits both utilized and developed. So be certain that you include interesting and challenging mental pursuits as requirements for the fulfillment of all of us. I would

love to visit an observatory, which you have never taken the time to do. Yes, watching Star Trek is intriguing, but it would also be nice to actually work on a project where we need to learn vast amounts of information. Remember, stretching the mind is a type of exploration and it's fun for me.

8. *LAINE, THE EXPLORER:* Boy, did you wimp out! The rest of you guys just didn't keep up on our trip to Bali. Where was all that energy anyway? I thought we'd never get to go anywhere again. You nearly died. Ugh. What a bore! So, yes, by all means, as long as we get to go to some exotic places and really see them, not just hang out in some snazzy hotel. I liked sleeping in the open-air pagoda in Bali. At least I got to move us along a little on the trip. You might not have even walked in the rice fields if it hadn't been for me. Memories are made from extraordinary happenings, not just sipping tea in the parlor. So I'm willing to cooperate as long as there is some adventure for me to get my teeth into. At least every six months, I want some adventure! Got it?

9. *BRYANT, THE TYCOON:* With regard to making money, non-profit agencies are not profitable. Boy, did you get yourself off course. Where's the money, kiddo? Yes, I'm the one who flashes the dollar signs in your mind for you to equate time with money. We just have got to get this show on the road. I like the scenario, and I want to see some action. Let's use the more dynamic, outgoing members of the team to get us out there to meet the right people, to get us into the bucks, energy flow, whatever you want to call it. The bottom line is bread in the hand, money in the bank. Sure I'm disgusted. It's been so long since you've used your business brain that we nearly went brain-dead. I want to own property that makes money. We've got a long way to go, but since I've got to hang in here until the show is over, I'm more than willing to get the engines revved-up so we can take off.

10. *MARTHA, THE MOTHER:* It is a crying shame that we never took the time to have children. I love them so very much. I enjoy watching them develop and am continuously amazed at how quickly their personalities become apparent. In the scenario, you talk about having children in our life. That is very important to me. It would be ideal to

have them in my own home and to raise a family; but if that is not possible, then I would like very much to have them as friends that visit often. I'd also like to help bring love to many children of the world. I want to care for and nurture and have fun with the child in everyone, even our dear Soleil, our child within. I am available with my own love of humanity to help in any way possible to make our life truly delightful and worthwhile.

11. *SOLEIL OF THE SUN:* I've been having a wonderful time these past few days. It seems like our first vacation in years. I love the swimming pool and laying in the sun, and I like to be out in the garden. I love watching the sunrise and don't even mind meditating in the morning. Oh, yes, I liked watching all those movies these past few days too. Nothing too serious, just fun. I'll go along with the scenario as long as there's time out for me to play. I want to sing and dance and enjoy myself. Let's not be too somber, all right, Bryant or Helena? You two do get carried away. I think it would be nice to play the harp and to take tai chi lessons again. Fun is important you know. See how it has helped you to clear up your brain? Don't forget. I like to play!

12. *HELENA OF THE HIGH COUNTRY:* The new scenario is interesting, but what I ask for is time alone without interruption. I love to be able to spend time meditating and opening to my spiritual awareness. I like to hike in the mountains and stroll along the seashore, alone, so my thoughts are my own. I even love traveling alone, so all the scenery and events are absorbed totally and not confused with the impressions of those close to me. I like to write my thoughts in the form of books and articles and choose to do so without worrying about critics. The scenario is fine as long as I have plenty of time to be alone. I don't want to be swept up in endless activity and social affairs. Give me time to think and rejuvenate, and I will go along with the scenario.

Well, I feel as if I've been taken through the car wash and cleaned up a bit. It is amazing the variety of viewpoints that can be in one person, and there are probably more. As captain of this crew and representative of this circle of varying needs and desires, I will read this material every day for two weeks and then often thereafter.

There are a lot of changes to be made in my outward persona to accomplish the scenario—some classes to take, some additional reading, and certainly some activities, meetings, gatherings and functions that I will need to attend to accomplish this.

I appreciate all of you sharing your viewpoints at this time. Please keep me informed of any ideas that come to mind to help in this new scenario. To shift one's life is only possible if all of one's self is heading in the same direction. If each wants to chart a different course, we end up going nowhere. Let's work on this project together and perhaps we can help others, as we help ourselves, to find their way in the midst of confusion.

Now ask the members of your crew to comment on the new scenario of your life which you have written.

CHAPTER 10

Using the Infusion Integration Technique

Who you are is often more complex,
more outrageous and more confusing
than you might want to consider.
Yet by looking, feeling, acting out,
and communicating with the various parts-of-you,
life can become harmonious and you can feel free.

Using the Infusion Integration Technique—learning to identify and clarify the various parts-of-me—has been an incredible adventure. I discovered that I often made decisions based on beliefs that were in conflict with other feelings and ideas inside of me. The conflicting beliefs were usually hidden from view. These discoveries led me to a new understanding of myself, and enabled me to put my life in order and balance by using Infusion.

In order to understand the Infusion Integration Technique, I will be illustrating numerous examples and giving you the wording, which can be used to integrate the parts-of-you who are holding different opinions about where you should go and who you should be.

Using the idea of the crew members on the sailing ship, you will see that getting to know all parts-of-you, even the most obscure, can be quite an adventure—well worth your time and energy.

HOW CAN WARTS ON YOUR HANDS BE DOING SOMETHING FOR YOU?

One of the first times I used Infusion with another person was with Monica, the seven-year-old daughter of a friend. I was visiting her parents when I noticed that Monica had big black warts all over her hands. They had just appeared a few days before. I asked her why she had the warts. What were they doing for her? She gave me a quizzical look and said she didn't know why. (I realize that asking why someone has a physical problem is not a normal question, but I have found that we usually know why. And the answer is often available to our conscious mind almost immediately if we simply ask the question.) So I asked Monica if she would play a little game with me. We would see if we could determine why she had the warts and perhaps get rid of them. She agreed to play the game.

I explained to Monica that a part-of-her must have created the warts for some reason. I asked her to choose one hand to represent the part-of-her who did not want warts, and the other hand would represent the part-of-her who had created the warts.

Monica chose the right hand to be the sub-personality which didn't want the warts, and her left hand was to represent the part-of-her who did want them for some reason. I touched the left hand and said, "Could you please tell me what you are doing *for* Monica by creating warts on her hands?"

Monica looked down at her hand and up at me. She seemed confused. "I don't know," she whispered.

"Let's think about it. Maybe the warts are stopping you from doing something. They seem to be stopping you from using your hands."

Monica thought a few minutes then answered, "Well, I fell off the monkey bars at school last week and got hurt."

"That might be it. Did you have trouble hanging on tightly?"

"Yes," she replied.

"With the warts on your hand you have an excuse not to climb on the monkey bars, don't you?"

"Yes," she said quietly.

"What if the warts could go away and you could play on the monkey bars and not fall off?"

"That would be okay," she answered.

"Good. Let's see if we can make that happen. Just close your eyes for a moment so we can get rid of the warts." She closed her eyes.

"Please ask the part-of-you who created the warts to go to the creative part-of-you and come up with three ways in which you can play on the monkey bars and not fall off. You don't need to know how this will happen.

"Now hold your hands up with the palms facing each other. Slowly bring your two hands together until they are touching."

Monica slowly brought her two little hands, covered in warts, together.

"Now, bring your hands up to your chest and imagine the two parts-of-you hugging each other. You will be able to play on the monkey bars without falling and the warts can go away. Thank you."

The next day the warts began to disappear from her hands. There was no need for a doctor to burn them off. They were simply re-absorbed by her body. From a mind/body connection point of view, the mind was now aware that the warts were not the only way to keep Monica from falling. As a child she may not have understood all the words I was saying, but many adults also don't understand all the words of the Infusion Integration Technique. What is important to note is that this method of reprogramming the mind and body seems to work effectively without needing to understand the process.

What we are maintaining through this example, and the many processes to follow, is that at various times, parts-of-you can make decisions which affect your life. Each of your sub-personalities thinks he or she is doing something for you by developing a solution to a problem. But this solution may just be creating a different problem.

Somehow, a member of the crew of this seven-year-old girl had heard of, seen or somehow conjectured that warts would be the solution to her not falling off the monkey bars. Without deliberation, and certainly without a visit to the creative part-of-her, a member of her crew decided that preventing her from using her hands was the best solution. When the possibility of another solution was offered, a solution that would be a win-win for all parts-of-her, the crew member decided to go along with the program and came up with new ways for Monica to play without falling.

FACING JEALOUSY AND FEELINGS OF INFERIORITY

Another example of looking closely at decisions we have made happened to me a number of years ago when I was challenged by my girlfriend, Barbara. One day, Barbara, John, my boyfriend, and I were sitting in the lovely lounge of a hotel in Carmel. Barbara announced loudly, "You know, Verlaine, I'm going to win!"

"What?" I asked. "I didn't know we were in a contest."

"I'm going to win John," she said.

I went into shock. John was my live-in boyfriend. We had been together for about eight years and had a loving relationship. I thought of Barbara as our mutual friend. We often went to dinner or to the movies as a threesome.

Barbara was quite beautiful with long blond hair and a great figure. She had a lovely voice and spoke several languages. She was intelligent, witty and charming. All of a sudden, I felt pangs of jealousy. A nauseating feeling arose within me. I felt I couldn't compete with Barbara. I knew this was silly. Upon appraisal of myself in the mirror, I could see that I was attractive; I felt intelligent and charming, not inferior. But it didn't seem to matter. I suddenly felt inferior to Barbara, and a feeling of jealousy arose.

I decided to use Infusion to find out what was going on inside of me. What member of my crew was causing feelings of not being good enough? I asked that part-of-me who was making me feel jealous to be represented by my left hand. And the one who felt confident and attractive was represented by my right hand.

(It really doesn't matter which hand you choose to represent the opposing parts-of-you. Yet it is interesting to note that the left hand corresponds to the right brain, which is more feeling oriented and intuitive. The right hand corresponds to the left brain, which is more verbal and logical.)

Remember, the idea is to allow yourself to become and act out that part-of-you that is being represented. Get into his or her point of view. You, the current conscious persona in charge, are the observer. If you do the process alone, naturally, it is the conscious you that will ask the questions, and the other parts-of-you will answer as if they are separate people. In many cases these sub-personalities will seem very different from each other and certainly different from you.

I asked the positive part-of-me: "What are the advantages of feeling confident and attractive?"

She replied, "It gives me the ability to tackle new projects, meet new people and feel good about my relationship with John. I have never felt jealous because I feel good about myself and enjoy people that are attractive and intelligent, whether they are men or women. I know John cares about me, and I don't have to worry about Barbara. If he would prefer to be with her, then I will naturally feel sad, but I know I will always have the love I need."

"Well, I guess that's extremely confident," I said. I then turned to the part-of-me who was feeling jealous and inferior and asked her to tell me what she was doing *for* me. She seemed rather shy and not very willing to talk.

Finally, she said, "Well, I'm not very pretty."

"What do you mean?" I asked. "How do you look? And, by the way, how old are you?"

(Sometimes, it can be helpful to know the age of the part-of-you who seems to be causing trouble. It is interesting to discover when you made the decision that is now upsetting you.)

"Well, I'm really a mess," she replied. "I wear glasses and have braces on my teeth and pimples on my face, and I'm overweight and wear dumb clothes. I'm fourteen."

"Oh, my," I said. "No wonder you're jealous and feel inferior. You're still caught in the old picture of myself when I was fourteen. Guess what? We've grown up! And we're not really a mess anymore."

"Easy for you to say," the fourteen-year-old part-of-me replied. "I can't compete with Barbara. I'm jealous of her."

"All right, I understand why you feel inferior," I replied. "What are you doing *for* me by maintaining this image of the fourteen-year-old who is not attractive?"

(Note: You must remember that these parts-of-you whom you will be contacting always think they are doing something *for* you. You may think they are punishing you or trying to upset you. That perspective is the other sub-personality's point of view. The part that is causing the problem, in this case the one creating the feeling of jealousy and inferiority, was trying to do something for me.)

"I'm keeping you from becoming proud and egotistical," she said. "If you remember your roots and know that you are really not attractive, then you'll be a good person and remain humble."

Notice the logic held by this part-of-me sounds similar to an oath, a decree, somewhat like a universal truth, which has been held as a belief. You will find that many of your beliefs are similar in their tone. It is the feeling, "but this statement is true," which sometimes makes it difficult to change our behavior.

"That's an interesting solution," I said. "What if there were a way I could be a good, humble person, and I still could feel confident and attractive without being proud and egotistical? If I could be what you've described, would you be willing to change your behavior and let the jealousy go?"

(Note: See how I wove all her considerations into the question? She wants me to be good and humble and not proud and egotistical. The other part-of-me wants to feel strong and confident. I just want to be free of the feeling of jealousy.)

My fourteen-year-old sub-personality responded, "I don't know if I can change."

"What else would you need in order to change your behavior and let me feel confident and attractive and let the jealousy go?" I asked.

"Well, I'd have to be certain that you would be kind to other people and understand when they don't feel attractive and confident."

"That seems fair. So if we add that to the list, are you willing to change your behavior and let me feel confident and attractive and let the jealousy go?"

"Yes," she replied.

"Good, I will now close my eyes and ask the fourteen-year-old part-of-me to now go to the creative part-of-me to come up with at least three ways in which I can feel confident and attractive and let go of the jealousy and, at the same time not be proud and egotistical. I will be a good person and humble and will also be kind to other people and understand when they don't feel attractive and confident. I would now like all parts-of-me to check those three ways to be certain that the solutions are a win-win for all parts-of-me.

"With my eyes closed, I hold my hands two feet apart, with the palms facing each other, and slowly bring the palms together until they are touching."

As I moved my hands together, I could see, in my mind's eye, the part-of-me who had maintained the age of fourteen, walking toward the older, more confident version of myself. As my palms touched, I saw the two hugging each other. Big tears fell from the eyes of the fourteen-year-old when she realized she no longer needed to feel ugly and inferior. I brought my hands, palms touching, up to my chest and held them there as I watched the scene in my mind's eye. I told the jealous part-of-me to see that the decision she had made was based on information she had available when she was fourteen. She is no longer alone and caught in the feeling of being unworthy. I told the two that were hugging that they were now one person, that they were no longer separate.

All parts-of-me were asked to form a huddle around the two in the center and direct love to them. Then I asked my Over Soul, my Higher Self, to hover over the two in the center, and to flow love through them and out to all parts-of-me. The energy of love is the glue of the universe and now that cohesive energy was healing all feelings of jealousy in my heart and mind.

I asked the two, the fourteen-year-old and the grown-up version of me, to go walking hand in hand and share stories and information, as they began to realize that they were one.

I thanked the two for sharing in consciousness. I asked all parts-of-me to share with me when they have concerns or requirements that are not being met appropriately.

After completing the Infusion Integration Technique, the feelings of jealousy subsided, and I continued directing love toward Barbara. Over the next few weeks I saw her a few times in town and I felt no animosity toward her. Within two months, she was offered a job in another city. She moved away, and I never saw Barbara again.

When we are feeling jealous or inadequate because of the way we look, it is important to remember that feeling beautiful and being radiant are not necessarily directly related to the beauty contestant or the model image we see in magazines or on television. When people get to know us, they are more likely to feel our inner beauty than they are to judge us by our actual physical features.

In college, I remember a young man who was very homely and whose face was deeply scarred from a severe complexion problem. At first sight, he appeared to be very unattractive. Yet, after getting to know him, anyone could see there was an intense inner beauty and a wonderful personality, which made him a delight to be around. Because he was able to project love, sensitivity and humor so wonderfully to his friends, he was constantly showered with hugs and kisses by the women who knew him.

Conversely, I have met many women and men with only skin-deep beauty. They project such a coldness-of-heart that heads are turned away when they come in the room. Beauty is not only in the eyes of the beholder. Beauty is also in the heart and personality of the one we behold.

Many times, when you are talking to the parts-of-you who are causing upset, anger or jealousy, you may discover that those sub-personalities are still young children or teenagers. They are often caught at an age when you began to hold a certain belief or picture about yourself, other people or events. These pictures or beliefs keep repeating until you discover what they are doing *for* you. There is no need to remain caught in a past picture. All past pictures are like old video tapes. They can be erased and/or changed.

You have the ability to change your life by changing your mind. You can reverse the effects of all that has happened to you by determining the advantages and benefits of past events. Often people cannot think of any advantages or benefits. We have been led to believe it is impossible for an accident, child abuse, a difficult financial experience, divorce, etc., to do something for us. By changing our perspective, perhaps we can imagine that at least one benefit of hardship is having the opportunity to learn compassion and deep understanding. If we have learned how to survive difficult times, we can empathize with many other people who have experienced similar difficulties. Through our learning of compassion, we may join the helping professions, become teachers, or simply act as good friends.

Many people talk about growing up in dysfunctional families. Yet, when I look at those people, I quite often see warm, loving, kind, aware and open individuals who are inclined to make the effort to learn about themselves, about family relationships and social interaction. What does a dysfunctional family experience do *for* an individual? It may create a person who seeks answers to buried questions and searches for healing techniques. It may create a counselor who decides to use some of his or her time and energy to help others.

The point of the Infusion Integration Technique is that you do not need to remain dysfunctional. Yes, that happened—the event—whatever it is or was. And maybe many events happened. It is time to complete those experiences in your mind and move on. It is time to clear the problem and find a better solution and a more beneficial behavior that will allow you to live a full and harmonious life. You can be free of feelings which limit your capabilities, if you will ask the part-of-you who is creating the feelings: "What are you doing *for* me?" And listen closely to the answers.

CHAPTER 11

Calling Forth
Wealth and Abundance

*Looking for wealth in our lives
can lead us to discover
an overwhelming abundance in nature.*

Y ou may have noticed there are a large number of people who do
not allow themselves to experience wealth and abundance. You
may be one of them. Why not? What is the part-of-you (that crew
member) doing for you who is saying "no" to abundance and wealth?
This is an exciting subject since our society has so effectively created
the idea that money is necessary, yet somehow evil. Winning the
lottery would be wonderful, but being rich could be a negative
experience. You see an example of negative rich people on television
shows, such as *Dallas*. The rich people are frequently the "bad guys."
You know how they got their money—through thievery or worse.
Right? Right!

If, in your new scenario, you wrote that you would like to have
wealth and abundance, it is very important to take the time to talk to
that part-of-you, the notorious crew member who has been blocking
wealth and abundance from your life. If you don't have the wealth you
want, or you're feeling guilty about wealth you already have, read on.

If you are already wealthy and happy about your wealth, you
don't need to read this section, but it might be helpful to understand
all those other people who were not born into money, didn't inherit it,

marry it, steal it or win the lottery. Forgive us, these methods of receiving money are what the non-wealthy people often believe are the only ways to become wealthy.

For all the people who would like to be wealthier and experience greater abundance, or not feel guilty (or want to help their poor friends), read on. It is important to begin by asking the part-of-you to step forward who believes she or he is doing something for you by keeping you poor, or just barely hanging on, or with just enough, but never too much money.

(Note: When you are doing this process and other Infusion Integration processes, it can be helpful to write down all the reasons the parts-of-you are expressing so you can repeat these considerations when you send them to the creative part-of-you.)

Begin by asking the part-of-you who wants to be wealthy and live abundantly to choose one hand to represent him or her. The part who feels that wealth and abundance are not appropriate is the other hand.

Let's ask each of these parts-of-you to respond by talking to each part and making a list of their reasons or beliefs in each category.

First, ask that part-of-you who wants to have wealth and abundance to make a list of the reasons for being wealthy. The following is a list of possible reasons to want free-flowing wealth:

- Money means freedom.
- Wealth brings security.
- Abundance would create peace of mind.
- Lots of money would give me a chance to travel.
- With wealth I could buy a lovely home.
- I could buy what I want when I want.
- If I were wealthy, I could help others.
- I would have the money to start beneficial projects.
- If I didn't have to work for a living, I could create art, music, drama, inventions, etc.
- I would have more time for enjoyable recreation.
- I could partake of my favorite sports.
- I could relax whenever I want.

Now, write down your reasons for wanting to be wealthy. Add your ideas and/or modify the list above.

Next, ask that part-of-you who does not want wealth and abundance to list the reasons (beliefs you might hold) for not being rich. Remember, these reasons are what being without wealth is doing *for* you. Here are some possible considerations for not wanting money:

- I 'm free of the extra responsibility that money might bring.
- Without wealth, people aren't jealous of me.
- I know people like me for myself, not because I have money.
- I'm free because I don't have a lot of things to worry about.
- The trappings of money may become entrapments.
- I earn my living. I don't want to work even harder to get rich.
- I can live a simple life. Money might corrupt me.
- I'm on a spiritual path, which means I shouldn't be rich.
- I like to live close to my roots.
- I don't want to become egotistical.
- I might become lazy and not accomplish anything.
- Rich people aren't happy. Money doesn't make you happy.

Now make your list of reasons for not wanting to be wealthy and/or modify the list above. Allow yourself the time to assume the role and the point of view of that part-of-you who thinks he or she is doing something for you by keeping you in a non-wealthy state physically and perhaps mentally and emotionally.

If you think that there is no part-of-you who does not want to be rich, then look around you and see if you have enormous wealth and abundance. If you do, you've mastered this exercise. And, as we said in the beginning of this wealth process, you are studying this material to try to understand why other people block monetary abundance. If you are not wealthy, it is likely that some part-of-you is holding beliefs about wealth, which are preventing you from receiving large sums of money. It is up to you to take the time to consider what those ideas might be. What are the beliefs you hold about wealth and money?

One of my beliefs, in the past, was "People might not like me if I were rich." I thought about that concept and realized maybe there were some people who didn't like me as I was, without money. Money wasn't a measure of whether or not people like me. So I might as well let money come to me.

Money is just energy, frozen green energy. It is simply a tool to exchange value. That is all it is. It cannot guarantee happiness, and it cannot make you unhappy. Happiness is up to you. Happiness is how you feel about what's happening now. Too many people believe happiness is something outside themselves, and thus money, and/or love, and/or something will make them happy. We cannot pursue happiness. Happiness is within us. We either like what's happening now or we don't. The only way to move from happiness to unhappiness and back to happiness is to change your point of view. You can change your perspective and opinion about what's happening, and then decide to be happy or not.

After you have made your two lists (1) why it is beneficial to be wealthy and (2) why it is better not to be wealthy, we can proceed with the Infusion process.

Now ask the part-of-you who does not want to be wealthy (who thinks it is doing something for you by keeping you from being rich): "What if there were a way you could have all the benefits on your list? Would you be willing to change your behavior and allow me to have wealth and abundance?"

If the non-wealthy part-of-you says no, or if there is hesitation, ask if there is some consideration that your non-wealthy crew member needs to add to the list. For instance, another consideration might be: "Well, if I were going to be wealthy, I wouldn't want to feel burdened," or "If I had abundance, I wouldn't want to feel like all my family and friends were trying to get at my money," or "I want to be sure I can have love in my life. I don't want money to get in the way of love."

"Fine, we understand. If you could have all the considerations you have just mentioned and the list you have made and any other considerations you may not have thought about at this time, would you be willing to let me have wealth and abundance?"

"Yes. I think so."

(Note: Even a tentative yes or maybe is satisfactory, but you might check to be certain that all considerations have been satisfied.)

"Can you think of anything else you might need?"

"No."

"Good. We'll proceed. I will now ask you to close your eyes."

Say the following: "I ask that part-of-me, who has believed it was doing something for me by not having wealth and abundance, to now go to the creative part-of-me, the part-of-me filled with an infinite supply of creative solutions."

(Note: After you have read the information, it is good to experience this area of the Integration Technique with your eyes closed. One suggestion is to read the material onto a tape and play it back for yourself.)

"Now that I am talking to the creative part-of-me, I will come up with at least three ways in which I can have wealth and abundance and feel freedom and security. I do not need to know what those three ways are in consciousness at this time."

(Note: Repeat the two lists to fulfill the needs of both parts-of-you. It's nice to combine the lists into sentences that flow in such a way as to make you feel as if it is happening now.)

For example, "The creative part-of-me will come up with at least three ways in which I can have wealth and abundance, and

- I can experience peace of mind.
- I can travel to beautiful places and live in a lovely home.
- I can buy what I want and help others in many wonderful ways.
- I can start projects and invest in art, antiques, music, etc.
- I can have time for enjoyable recreation, including my favorite sports, and relax whenever I want to.
- at the same time, I 'm free of the extra responsibility that money might bring.
- people aren't jealous of me. In fact, they are happy for me.
- people like me for myself, not because I have money.
- I feel free, and I don't have to worry about the things I own.
- I never feel trapped by my wealth and abundance.
- my life becomes easier, and I don't have to work harder to have wealth and abundance.
- I can live a simple life if I want to, and I see that wealth helps me, it doesn't corrupt me.
- I have more time for spiritual study.
- I can give money to those less fortunate than myself.
- I can live close to my roots and won't become egotistical.
- I won't become lazy. Instead I will accomplish many wonderful things. Yet I know how to relax.
- I feel at ease and don't feel burdened by my wealth.

- my family and friends treat me wonderfully.
- friends don't act as if they are trying to get at my money.
- I have love in my life and money never gets in the way of love.
- I live in a state of happiness and peace, with or without money. My wealth and abundance is simply the icing on the cake. The cake is my state of happiness. The wealth and abundance just add to it.

"Now, we ask all my sub-personalities to check those three ways and make certain that these are win-win solutions for all parts-of-me. Again, I do not need to know what those three ways are in consciousness at this time.

"I hold my two hands about two feet apart with the palms facing each other. I see the wealthy part-of-me facing the crew member who thought she was doing something for me by keeping me free of wealth. She had made her decisions based upon the information available to her at the time. Now I will see myself acting differently, allowing wealth and abundance to flow to me.

"Slowly, I bring my hands together until they are touching. I see the two embracing each other. The unwealthy part-of-me, who was afraid that I would be corrupted by being wealthy, is hugging the more secure, wealthy part-of-me. I allow the feelings to flow between them knowing that each one thought they were doing something for me as they battled endlessly about who was right.

"With the palms still touching, I bring my two hands up to my chest. My left hand lays flat over my heart and the right one rests over the back of the left hand.

"I see the two beginning to blend into one. I am the loving, grown-up person who can now enjoy the ability to experience wealth and abundance. I see all parts-of-me forming a huddle around the two in the center and directing love to them, healing them.

"My Higher Self is hovering overhead, sending love, wisdom and healing to the two parts who are becoming one. The energy of my Higher Self, my Over Soul, the spiritual part-of-me, is healing the two who were so opposite in their opinions about wealth and abundance.

"I see the two walking hand in hand, sharing concepts and ideas, updating the information available to them about how they can live in harmony and help to create the abundance they can both enjoy.

"I thank you for sharing in consciousness at this time. Let it be known that I will listen and be available to do the Infusion Integration Technique with any sub-personality who may need help or assistance. And I thank you."

(Note: You will notice that we suggest that the two become one. Then we say, "See the two walking hand in hand, sharing concepts and ideas." Even though they have blended, it takes a little time for the two to completely agree, come to a consensus and absorb the three solutions from the creative part-of-you. Seeing them walking and sharing information is a nice way to facilitate that coming together without creating the feeling of forcing them to do so.)

What happens after you have done this process? You will see yourself acting, thinking and feeling differently. You will notice that your behavior, and the behavior of others toward you, seems to change. And you will find that new opportunities or unusual experiences may begin to happen. Interesting, wealth-producing ideas may begin to formulate as you move toward your new comfort level of being at ease with wealth and abundance.

How long will it take to become wealthy and have abundance? It can be weeks or months, possibly years, but you can be certain that you will begin to change your relationship to wealth almost immediately. You may begin by living in a wealthy environment without having wealth yourself.

My experience of this new relationship to wealth was to change jobs six months after doing the Infusion Integration Technique. During that six months, I found myself feeling more comfortable with the idea of wealth. Before I had used the Infusion Technique, I thought wealthy people were not good people. I thought all the problems of society should have been mended by those with wealth. I had a very limited concept of what it meant to be wealthy, and I had equated wealth with selfishness. In the Infusion process, I asked: "What if wealthy people could be generous, kind, good people? Therefore, I could be a generous, kind, good, wealthy person."

Shortly after doing the Infusion process, I began to meet very nice, kind, generous, wealthy people. It was a big surprise.

At the end of the six months, I left my job as Director of a Chamber of Commerce in a small town to become Director of Sales at a beautiful resort hotel, the Lodge at Pebble Beach. At the hotel, I had signing privileges to take conference leaders to lunch or dinner at all the lovely restaurants and the Beach Club and became accustomed to riding in a Rolls Royce. I began to live the life of a millionairess, even though I was paid a very modest salary.

At Pebble Beach, I found that there were many conferences being held by wealthy people who were trying to find solutions to society's problems. Another big surprise.

The movement toward wealth and abundance has been slow but steady for me. I have repeated the Infusion process on many occasions, and have uncovered many reasons (beliefs and decisions) that I had held, which kept me from becoming wealthy. It is worth the time and effort to do this exercise to release your energy, and to fully enjoy life and all that it has to offer.

It is interesting to note that less than five years after doing the Infusion Integration Technique, I was earning over $100,000 per year and had over $100,000 in savings. I was vice president of a high technology company. I had sold one company for a $40,000 personal profit and had sold a house for $60,000 profit. These opportunities had come to me because I had a more expansive, confident self-impression. I did not have a college degree, yet I was working with Ph.D's from top universities. It was very exciting and rewarding. The change was truly amazing.

Five years later, I had become lax in my use of Infusion. I had begun to believe in the inflation mentality of the 1980s. I was successful, but exhausted. I wanted more meaning, more friends, more love in my life. I began to go through my mid-life crisis. I quit my job, spent the money in the bank and went into debt.

Within two years, I fell down the steps in a movie theater and then lost nearly everything: my home, my business, my health, my romantic relationship. Needless to say, I had to look again at the beliefs I was holding. What were the beliefs that allowed those disastrous events to take place?

For some reason, I had neglected to realize I had two very powerful beliefs: (1) I must always work hard for my money, or it would disappear, and (2) holding money in savings is silly.

There was a freedom-loving sub-personality that just wanted to spend and travel. She took control of the ship, and she would no longer pay any attention to my business sub-personality. The freedom-loving crew member made wild decisions. She traveled, invested in the movie production and paid the expenses of other people. Deep within me I discovered I held another unproductive concept: "Being a wealthy woman meant I had to take care of everyone around me."

So I asked the one who wanted to take care of everyone, "What if you could be wealthy and you didn't have to take care of everyone around you? What if you could be taken care of instead?" This was a totally different concept.

(Note: You will notice that in the Infusion Wealth Exercise, we asked the unwealthy part-of-you, "If you could have all the considerations you have just mentioned, the list you have made and any other considerations you may not have thought about at this time, would you be willing to let me have wealth and abundance?" This is a key phrase: "and any other considerations you may not have thought about at this time." By including this concept, your subconscious and all your sub-personalities can throw in their considerations, such as my thinking that I must take care of everyone around me if I were wealthy. By using this phrase, you are making and including all considerations in the exercise. Hopefully, you will not have to wait as long as I did, continuously searching for the blockages. I hope you won't have a boomerang hit you, as I did, when one of my crew members thought my best growth would come from losing everything.)

I must say, I did grow tremendously through my losses, and I am grateful for that growth; but I do believe that we can grow in joy and peace and harmony. We don't always have to knock our heads against a wall to wake up. We can be alert, awake, aware, wealthy and we can grow, be free, in love and at peace. We can have it all.

CHAPTER 12

The Infusion Process

*The process of integrating your sub-personalities
can lead to the integration of your heart, mind and soul.*

The Infusion Integration Technique can be used in many ways to help you to manifest your desires, realize your goals and create peace and harmony in your relationships. I have found the Infusion Technique to be an all-purpose tool that can assist you in handling large events and the everyday problems of life. This chapter is designed to provide you with the primary structure and key phrases to use in doing the Infusion process.

1. Begin the Infusion Integration Technique by identifying your problem. Be specific and write down what is bothering you, such as:
    you need money
    you don't feel healthy
    you'd like to change careers
    you're not expressing your creativity
    you're not in a meaningful relationship
    you feel depressed, angry, sad or upset
    you're not manifesting your heart's desires.

2. Quiet your mind and ask to speak to the two parts-of-you who are in conflict. One part-of-you wants to be wealthy, healthy, in love, change careers, etc. The other part-of-you is stopping you because he or she may want you to learn through hard work or make you rest by

getting sick. A part-of-you may want to avoid love so you can be free or stay in the same career to be safe, etc.

3. In order to divide the two parts-of-you, it is easiest to use your hands to represent each of the conflicting sub-personalities. Choose one hand to represent the part-of-you who wants wealth, health or love. The other hand will represent the part-of-you who is trying to protect you by stopping the wealth, health or love. You (your primary consciousness) will be an observer and listen as these two opposing parts-of-you give reasons for their positions and opinions.

4. Turn first to the part-of-you who wants money, love, health, etc., and ask: "What are the advantages of being wealthy or healthy or in love? How would you benefit by having what you want?" Let this part-of-you tell you the advantages. Write them down.

5. Next turn to the part-of-you who is creating the problem or stopping you in some way and ask: "What are you doing *for* me? What are the advantages of experiencing a lack of money, feeling unhealthy or living alone? Are you trying to help me in some way?"

Often this part-of-you thinks he or she is protecting you from some sort of danger—physical, mental or emotional. Listen closely to discover what might be the underlying belief that has created this point of view. (For example, underlying beliefs can be: "If I'm rich, people will be jealous," or "The only time to rest is when I'm sick," or "Committed relationships are too confining.") Let this part-of-you talk. Write down a list of reasons this part-of-you thinks are advantages of living a simple life, having health problems or being alone.

6. After making the list of why you should be stopped or pro- tected, ask the protective part-of-you, "What if there were a way that all your considerations could be satisfied? Would you be willing to change your behavior and let me have the positive things I want?"

(Examples of statements that would combine considerations with desires are: "What if there were a way you could be wealthy and people would not be jealous of you?" or "What if you could take time to rest without needing to become sick?" or "What if you could have a committed relationship and still feel free?") Often this part-of-you will say it is impossible to have all the considerations he or she wants and at the same time be able to satisfy the desires of the opposing part-of-you who wants money, health or love.

7. If this protective part-of-you finds it difficult to agree, ask "What else do you need in order to let me have what I desire?"

The protective part-of-you may believe you need to be humble or you need to work hard so you don't become lazy. After all the considerations have been mentioned, ask again: "If all these considerations could be satisfied, would you be willing to change your behavior and let me be wealthy, healthy or in a relationship, etc.?"

When you reach agreement—a "Maybe" will do—then continue. (It is best to close your eyes when you do the following section. You can memorize these words or put the phrases on tape.)

8. Now close your eyes and send the part-of-you who has been stopping you to the creative part-of-you. Imagine the creative part-of-you to be a beautiful room filled with golden light. In this room is an incredible computer which can solve any problem in the universe.

Ask the creative part-of-you to come up with at least three ways in which all your considerations on this matter can be met and you can also have what you desire. You do not need to know what those three ways are in consciousness at this time. You will just see yourself acting differently and you will notice interesting coincidences that assist you. Ask all parts-of-you to check those three ways and make sure they are "win-win" solutions for all parts-of-you.

9. Now hold your hands up in front of you about two feet apart with the palms facing each other. In your mind's eye, see the two parts-of-you facing each other. See the one who has been wanting wealth, health or love, etc., facing the one who has been stopping you.

10. Slowly bring your two hands together until they are touching. See the two hugging and holding each other. See them merging into one. With the palms still touching, bring your hands up to your chest. Move the right hand over the left hand which should be resting over your heart.

11. Now see all parts-of-you forming a huddle around the two in the center, sending love and healing as they blend into one.

12. See your Higher Self hovering over you sending love and golden light to the two in the center and flowing down through all parts-of-your-being.

13. See the two parts-of-you walking hand in hand by a beautiful stream sharing concepts and ideas. See them sit down on a grassy hill bordered by lovely flowers and let them discuss how they will work together to create harmony and peace in your environment.

14. Thank these two for sharing in consciousness at this time. Let all parts-of-you know that you are available to listen and work with them to accomplish their goals in a positive way.

Sit quietly, float freely in your mind, and give your deeper self the opportunity to assimilate the new information which is beginning to work unconsciously within you. Rest easily and feel the positive shift inside of you.

Be aware of your feelings, relationships and environment. Be ready to talk to the parts-of-you who may need counseling and utilize the Infusion Integration Technique to change your life.
You can use the Infusion Integration Technique whenever you feel upset, concerned or when something you desire is missing in your life. It will become a method of changing your mind and your life experience easily and quickly. Practice it several times a day and expect miracles.

CHAPTER 13

Clearing the Way
for Relationships

Your personal relationship is your closest mirror.
The man or woman in your life is acting out
all that you hold dear, beautiful and lovely,
or acting disgusting and driving you crazy.
How can you create a meaningful relationship?
Change yourself.

From the time we are small children and during our confusing teenage years, there is usually an abiding feeling we will one day meet the love of our lives, get married, have children and live happily ever after. All the fairy tales and children's stories help to perpetuate the concept that there is a special man or woman for us who will fulfill our dreams, and give us all we need in terms of love and attention.

So why doesn't it happen this way? If we do meet someone we think we are in love with, and if we either marry them or begin to live together as man and wife, very often (50% of the time in the United States) it doesn't seem to work out. There is either a divorce or separation.

I lived quite happily with one man for twenty years and during that time we watched our friends marry and divorce. And then one day he left. It was not totally a surprise. For three years he had been living in Europe six months of the year, and returned to be with me six months. Our relationship had become familial. We cared about each other in much the same way a sister and brother do. He was living the life he wanted, and I was developing a new way of life.

As I looked closely at the breakup of my relationship, I realized that I had been doing a lot of inner changing. I had been looking at what I really wanted and found I desired a committed personal relationship (meaning marriage) in which my partner would want to be with me (not be away six months of the year). I wanted him to make plans with me for the future. I wanted physical passion along with a strong mental connection. I wanted to make decisions as a couple about the home we would live in, the car we would drive, and where we would go on vacation. I wanted a complete personal relationship, not a business partnership. I wanted to be part of a couple who adored each other and were "wannabes," people who wanted to be together.

Using the Infusion Technique to resolve problems in all types of relationships—personal, professional, social and casual—is quite fascinating. I have found that as you change the part-of-you who is represented by a person outside of you—whether it is your mate, a person at work, a friend or relative—that person either changes or is no longer in your life.

Let me explain. This is a stretch of the imagination but it is worth the exercise. The concept is: every person in your life is a representation of a part-of-you. Your friends, family and co-workers all act out your sub-personalities for you. They are the outer representation of the pirate crew we have been talking about.

You might respond to me by saying, "You're crazy. There's no way that I'm that sloppy, stuck-up, mean, silly, stingy, extravagant, etc."

Yet this theory maintains that every person, no matter how much he or she doesn't seem to be a part-of-you, is showing you a sub-personality within you that you may not want to recognize. Often the person outside of you is acting out the role in an extreme.

These parts-of-you, showing up in the form of other people outside of you, say the things you don't want to hear. They are the actors on the stage of your life acting out for you, so you can see what you are thinking, feeling and believing.

Each person in your life may represent only a small part-of-you, but they often act out whatever is bothering you in extremes. It is as though your deeper mind magically magnetizes the minds of those around you to act out what you have denied or hidden from yourself. Yet once you identify what they are doing for you and integrate that service into yourself, they will either change their behavior toward you, or they will no longer be in your life.

This may sound like a radical solution, but I have seen it work hundreds of times. If you will do the peace-making integration process inside of you, the people in your life will actually change their behavior toward you. These people who were bothering you may continue to treat others in the same way as in the past, but they no longer will bother you—because you have already acknowledged their message. They no longer need to play that role for you. These bothersome people will either change their behavior toward you or they will no longer be a major part of your life.

CHANGING RELATIONSHIPS BY CHANGING YOUR THOUGHTS

An example of changing a relationship in a positive way in the work environment was demonstrated to me when a new lady manager (we'll call her Susan) came to work in my office. On the very first day, Susan started yelling at me about my incorrect rendition of a logo color. It was not quite the right hue of red. I maintained that very few people would see the logo, and our deadline had passed for changing the color on that particular poster. She got angrier and yelled louder in front of our mutual boss. I was very surprised by her behavior.

I went home that evening and began to ask the part-of-me she represented (according to this concept she was acting out a sub-personality within me), "What is she doing for me?"

The first time you ask this question, especially when another person is involved, it is often confusing. The mind wants to argue, "What do you mean doing something for me? She isn't doing anything for me. She's acting crazy. She just yelled for no good reason."

So, you ask again, gently, "I would like to speak to my sub-personality who is represented by Susan. What were you doing *for* me by displaying that type of behavior and yelling at me about such a small problem? What is your underlying belief?"

The Susan part-of-me represented answered, "I'm showing you, one more time, that in order to be a good manager you have to pay attention to details. You've got to be a perfectionist in all that you do. I believe what's worth doing, is worth doing well." (I remember my father saying this statement many times as I was growing up.)

There was my answer. Susan was representing the macho, lady executive, perfectionist part-of-me. And this sub-personality yelled at me through Susan for being sloppy. Yes, it is a fact that sometimes there are parts-of-you whom you do not like. But if you can take the time to truly look inside, you will find that you, too, may have yelled at someone or wanted to, about their not doing the type of job you wanted them to do. So you also have a perfectionist inside of you.

I then asked that macho, lady executive, perfectionist part-of-me, "If there were a way that I could do a good job, if I could do things well and pay attention to details, and you no longer needed to yell at me, inside or outside of me, would you be willing to change your behavior and let me relax as I accomplish my work?"

She replied: " Yes, as long as you do things well!"

I then asked the Susan part-of-me to go to the creative part-of-me to come up with three ways in which I could: do a good job, pay attention to details, do my work efficiently, and be relaxed. I wouldn't be yelled at, nor would I have any problems with my co-workers.

I asked all my sub-personalities to check those three ways to make certain that the solutions were a win-win for all parts-of-me. I placed my hands two feet apart and slowly brought them together. In my mind's eye, I saw the Susan part-of-me, dressed in her proper business suit, slowly moving toward the relaxed, feminine, nonbusiness part-of-me until they met. I saw them hug each other and blend into one.

I brought my hands, with the palms touching, up to my chest and watched all parts-of-me forming a huddle around the two in the center. I saw the radiant energy of my Higher Self hovering overhead, directing love to the two and flowing out to all parts-of-me.

I saw the two sub-personalities walking hand in hand, sharing concepts and ideas, realizing they had been operating with limited information. They could each be good at business without feeling anxious or burdened. They could allow the feminine part-of-me to feel alive and well, even in an office environment. I thanked them for sharing in consciousness at this time.

Guess what happened? No, Susan did not quit. Her office was next to mine; and, even though we were often on the premises at the same time, I didn't have one opportunity to talk to her for the next two months. I would pass her in the corridor, and we would say hello to each other, but we had no significant interaction. With her bad temper, she caused a lot of chaos for others in the office, often for no apparent reason. Yet, over the next nine months, she was always pleasant to me. She never attacked me again in any way. I no longer needed her to act out aggression for me in that way.

Do I maintain that every person who acts aggressively toward you is acting out your inner aggression for you? Yes! I know this concept won't necessarily make you happy. You probably won't like this idea, because it is so easy to dislike the person who is performing this role for you. But the advantage of this theory is that you can change the behavior of others toward you by changing yourself.

Another example: I was working in a start-up, high-tech company in Northern California. The pressure of the venture capitalists and a new, unproven product needing to go to market was a very stressful experience. Everyone was working long hours, sometimes all night, trying to develop and complete the product. Our high-pressure investors were very dissatisfied with the software developers' progress. One day the sun was shining beautifully, and I suggested to three co-workers that we go to an outdoor restaurant down the street and have lunch. They agreed.

When we arrived in the patio of the restaurant, I decided that we should take down the umbrella over the table so we could feel the sun on our backs. As I started to fiddle with the umbrella, the owner of the restaurant came running across the patio, screaming at the top of his voice, "How dare you destroy my restaurant! The nerve of you to wreck my restaurant!"

I looked at him in shock and sat down quietly. Now, our normal reaction to this type of event is to say to ourselves and our friends, "Wow, what's wrong with him? He must have gotten up on the wrong side of the bed! Maybe he had a fight with his wife. Maybe business is bad, etc." But this new view proposes a truly magical and mystical universe which responds as a mirror to yourself.

Because I knew about the Infusion Integration Technique, I said to myself, "Wow, Verlaine, look at how angry you are!" This idea is a very different approach to interaction with other people. No matter what is happening, you must understand that the feeling, action, idea or belief is inside of you in order to create the event outside of you. The event, action, words or behavior could not show up in front of you if they were not inside of you. They are showing up for a reason, and it's usually related to how you are thinking and feeling.

I looked at the anger of the restaurant owner and realized, yes, I had built up a lot of anger inside of me. I was angry about the stress at my job. I felt resentment about not being supported, personally and professionally. I had not expressed, nor had I acknowledged, this anger in any way. I had held it all tightly bottled within me.

I went home and hit pillows with my fists. I kicked the pillows around the room. I went for a run around the block and yelled out all the feelings that were bothering me. When I was finished, I relaxed, and let the feelings of anger and upset fly away. The next day I went to the office and talked to the other employees about what was bothering me, and we were able to clear up a number of misunderstandings. After this event, the days and weeks passed without any displays of anger showing up outside of me (for the anger was no longer inside of me).

Every event, activity and conversation can be your opportunity to learn more about yourself, and you can make the necessary attitude adjustments. By utilizing Infusion you can help create new behavior and new events. The sub-personality who thought it was doing something for you will be able to accomplish his or her goal without causing the anger, upset, frustration, fear or pain. It will no longer need to attract your attention by creating negative events in your life.

YOU CAN CREATE A MEANINGFUL, LONG-LASTING, LOVING PERSONAL RELATIONSHIP

After all this discussion of general relationships, it is important to talk about what many people seem to be striving for: a personal, meaningful, long-lasting, loving relationship. If you are presently in such a wonderful personal relationship, then I suggest that you begin writing a book or teaching workshops to help the ninety percent of the people who don't seem to have achieved your success. If you are not in a wonderful personal relationship, then read on. This section also applies to people who are currently in a relationship, but the relationship is not ideal.

Through using the Infusion Integration Technique, you may find that there has been confusion in your mind about personal relationships. You may be having difficulties because a sub-personality, an obstinate crew member, still wants to be single and out of a relationship. Therefore, the single part-of-you is helping to create difficulties, arguments, disagreements, outrageous temptations and other problems so you will once again be free.

It is important to remember that a personal relationship is not the total answer to experiencing happiness in your life. Many people think the emptiness they feel will be filled when that special person enters their lives. Some individuals want a partner to generate the happiness they are unable to feel. A personal relationship is not designed to make you feel whole. It is a celebration when two people feel complete in themselves and are ready to share love in a growing relationship.

Let's assume there is a sub-personality within you that would like to be in a marvelous personal relationship. And there is another part-of-you who does not like the idea and is doing something for you by keeping you out of a meaningful, long-lasting, loving personal relationship, or by making the relationship you are in more difficult. Yes, there is a sub-personality within you, a crew member, who is a loner and who is keeping you out of a personal relationship.

We will begin by asking the relationship part-of-you to be represented by one hand. The loner part will be the other hand. You'll be the observer as these two sub-personalities discuss points of view.

Addressing the relationship part-of-you: "What are the advantages of being in a personal relationship?" I will write down some possible answers. You fill in answers of your own.

The advantages of a meaningful, long-lasting, loving personal relationship are:

- I have someone with whom I can share my love.
- I have someone with whom to plan and share experiences.
- I have a person to wake up with in the morning.
- I have a feeling of being cared for and loved.
- I have a friend with whom I can grow old gracefully.
- I have a partner with whom I can share income and expenses.
- I have someone who will love me in spite of my faults.
- I have a supporter who encourages me to grow and develop.
- I have a romantic lover who gives me cards and presents.
- I have someone to love and to cherish.
- I make my mother or father pleased because I'm happy.
- I make my friends delighted because I'm in a relationship.

Now ask the part-of-you who does not want to be in a personal relationship, "What are the advantages of staying single and being without a personal relationship?" I will write down some possible answers. You fill in answers of your own.

The advantages of staying single and not putting myself in a personal relationship are:

- I'm free and don't have to report to anyone about what I am doing or planning to do.
- I can make my own decisions without consulting anyone.
- I can date many people and don't have to settle down into some kind of boring rut.
- I am free of responsibility.
- I can act any way I want and don't have to get along with someone else if I don't want to.
- I can annoy my parents or friends who think I should be in a committed relationship.
- I like being on my own.
- I don't have to be bored with the same person every day.

Add any ideas or beliefs from your sub-personality who likes to be single and maintain his or her free lifestyle.

Now ask the single part-of-you who likes not being in a personal relationship, "What if there were a way I could have all the considerations mentioned?"

- I could feel free and wouldn't have to report to anyone about what I am doing or planning, unless I wanted to.
- I could make my own decisions.
- I could feel the excitement in my relationship, as if I were dating many people. (After all, my partner will have his or her own crew with their many sub-personalities to get to know.)
- I won't have to feel like I've settled down into some kind of rut. Instead, my relationship can be fun and interesting all the time.

"What if I could have all these benefits I have mentioned of being single? Would I be willing to change my behavior and experience a personal relationship?"

The single part-of-you might agree or might have some other considerations he or she would like to add, such as: "As long as I don't feel as if I'm in prison. I want to feel free!"

"All right, what if I could feel free, definitely not in prison, and I still had the joy of sharing my life on an intimate basis with another person, would I be willing to change my behavior and experience a loving personal relationship?"

That part-of-you will probably say, "Yes" or "Maybe."

(Note: It's important to realize the assumption we are making throughout the use of the Infusion Integration Technique. The concept is saying that your own thoughts and behavior are creating the experiences you call reality. You are creating your anger, your loneliness, your aloneness and your sense of failure or success. Thus by changing your inner understanding and the beliefs you hold, you can change your behavior, which is often unconscious, and create the desires of your heart. Your decisions do not have to be an either/or proposition. You do not have to choose between love and freedom. You do not have to choose between wealth and happiness, work and an opportunity to rest, a job that pays well and a creative life. The

Infusion Integration Technique can help you to incorporate and bring into your life all the considerations you think are important.)

Are there any other considerations the single part-of-you would need fulfilled in order to allow you to be in a personal relationship?

If the single part-of-you says, "Those are all of my considerations," then continue. If there are more, then ask, "If that consideration could be handled, would you be willing to change your behavior?" Ask until there are no more considerations available in consciousness. Every consideration is important. Every thought, concept and belief is worth considering. (For example: I don't want to have to pick up my partner's clothes. I want life to be easy and fun. I want my partner to like the same hobbies and activities I do, etc.)

After looking closely for all considerations, then continue by saying, "I will now close my eyes (review this script and then close your eyes), and ask the single part-of-me to go to the creative part-of-me to come up with a minimum of three ways in which I can have all the considerations I have been holding for being single, and, at the same time, I can enjoy the benefits of a personal relationship. I do not need to know what those three ways are in consciousness at this time. I will just see myself acting differently and having new experiences which will lead me toward a personal relationship."

Now repeat all the benefits of a personal relationship and combine them with the benefits of being single. This repeating of the benefits helps both sub-personalities to realize they are joining together in the creative part-of-you to develop new behavior and experiences.

"Through this new behavior I will have all the benefits of a great relationship:

- I have a wonderful partner to share pleasant experiences.
- I see a delightful person when I awaken in the morning.
- We can plan our days, weeks and the years ahead together.
- I have a companion who cares for me.
- I have someone with whom to share love.
- I have a helpmate with whom I can grow old gracefully.
- My partner is my best friend who makes life special every day.
- I live with someone who loves me in spite of my faults.
- My partner gives me support and encouragement.
- My loving sweetheart gives me cards and presents.

- My partner loves and adores me.
- My relatives are happy for me.
- My friends are delighted for me about my relationship.

"At the same time, I have the benefits of being single:

- I feel free, and I don't feel as if I have to report to anyone about what I am doing or planning to do unless I want to.
- In many ways I like sharing my plans and desires with this person whom I love.
- I can make my own decisions without consulting anyone, and at the same time will enjoy sharing with my partner.
- I enjoy the company of other people, if I want to, and I don't feel restricted.
- I don't feel as if I've settled down into a rut, although I feel relaxed and at ease.
- My life with my partner is fun and interesting.
- I feel free of undue responsibility. I know responsibility simply means the ability to respond, and I am responsive and enjoy caring about my partner.
- I act any way I want, because I am able to be myself.
  - It is easy to live together, because we share so many joys.
- I make myself happy in this relationship.
- If others are happy for me, that is a pleasant addition to my life.
- I may enjoy the feeling of being on my own, if I want to, because I know that this partnership is not intrusive, but adds joy and pleasure to my life.
- I don't have to argue and fight in this personal relationship.
- I am understood and communicate easily with my partner.
- I am treated in a very special way in this relationship.
- I feel loved, cherished and adored.
- I enjoy the concept of long-lasting, because our time together is not boring. Our time is valuable and enjoyable.
- As I share more with my partner, we blend into one.

"I now ask all my sub-personalities to check three ways in which this can happen and make certain that these solutions are a win-win for all parts-of-me. Make certain I can now have a personal relationship, and at the same time will not lose my sense of feeling free. Again, I do not need to know what those three ways are in consciousness at this time. I will simply see myself acting differently and enjoying new experiences in the days and weeks ahead.

"Now, with my eyes closed, I hold my two hands two feet apart with the palms facing each other. I see, in my mind's eye, on one side of me, the partnership part-of-me who has been wanting a personal relationship. On the other side, I see the single part-of-me, who has believed that keeping me single meant helping me to be free from entanglements.

"As I slowly bring my two hands together, the two sub-personalities move toward each other until my hands are touching. The lonely crew member looks at the one who wanted to stay single and they hug each other. I see the two becoming one. The single part begins to understand that he or she had made my decision to stay single based on information available long ago. Now I have new information. I no longer need to feel hurt, afraid, lost and alone.

"All parts-of-me form a huddle around the two in the center and direct healing love to them. My Higher Self sends waves of love and golden-white, healing light down through the two in the center and out to all parts-of-me.

"The two crew members go walking hand in hand, sharing concepts and ideas and learning how to work together to create a loving relationship—first with each other, then with an intimate partner. At the same time, I can create joyful relationships with family, friends and associates.

"Let it be known to all my sub-personalities that they are welcome to express their needs and desires to me, and I will listen and help them to experience the Infusion Integration Technique. I thank you for sharing in consciousness."

After you have gone through an Infusion process, it is a good idea to allow yourself to rest and feel the shift inside of you. Sit quietly, float freely in your mind, and give yourself the opportunity to integrate the new information which is beginning to work in your unconscious. After you have used Infusion a number of times, you will find it is easy to go through the monologue. As you move your hands together, you will feel the different parts-of-you integrating very quickly.

You now have created an opportunity for the creative part-of-you to help you change your behavior. You will be more aware of events, activities and the people in your environment, which may lead you to a loving relationship. You will be prepared on a physical, emotional and mental level to share love—to experience the feeling of joy that can come from meeting a man or woman who can fulfill your desire for loving companionship.

At first, you may not notice a change in your behavior; but as the weeks pass, you may see yourself more interested in exercising, eating the right foods, reading books on self-improvement, talking to friends and hearing about relationships which are meaningful and long-lasting. People might start setting you up on dates, inviting you to parties, suggesting that you join classes, asking you to participate in sporting activities, all leading you toward meeting the man or woman who will become your loving partner.

At the same time, it is up to you to be open and willing to listen to any of your sub-personalities who may start putting up road blocks. After a month, if nothing new is happening in your life, if you do not feel any changes in your movement toward a lasting, loving relationship, go through the Infusion process again. Check to see if there are any considerations for being single that you didn't think about the first time. Listen closely to the statements of friends and relatives, especially those statements which bother you. Bothersome statements are usually buried deep within you, and a part-of-you may be magnetizing those thoughts into statements to be said by other people for you to hear.

An example of such a statement might be: Your mother says to you, "Why don't you wear something more attractive? Your sloppy shirt and stringy hair look terrible."

Normally, we respond to a negative statement from our mothers by saying, "What do you know? This is what everyone is wearing. I like my hair like this. Leave me alone!"

Let's take a look at this statement about the sloppy shirt. Perhaps one of your sub-personalities is speaking through your mother. This part-of-you is bringing to your attention that you are not showing your attractive body. You say you want a loving relationship, and you are dressing in a way which might turn off a potential partner. You are appearing as someone who does not care how they present themselves. You are giving an image of not liking yourself enough to dress attractively.

The remarks about the stringy hair may also be a part-of-you trying to prepare you to meet a partner. Your hair can be your crowning glory. It can enhance your face and make any clothes look more lovely. If your hair is clean and shiny, and you take the time to have it cut into a nice style, your whole appearance can be more attractive.

Another statement that you might not like could come from a friend after you turn down an invitation to go to a gathering: "You never go anywhere. You spend too much time alone. You better be careful or you'll always be single."

Look closely at the words. The part-of-you who wants to be in a loving relationship may have stimulated the words to come out of your friend's mouth for you to hear. (Remember, we're talking magic here.) You may not be bothering to listen internally to your sub-personality who believes you are not participating enough with people. That part-of-you may think you are spending too much time alone. You can do the Infusion process to find out what this part-of-you is trying to accomplish by keeping you alone.

What are the advantages of being alone? Perhaps he or she is protecting you from interacting with people who may not like you. Your sub-personality may be helping you to learn more about yourself by studying, reading, walking or being alone. He or she may be isolating you to prevent you from making a mistake and falling in love with the wrong person.

The alone part-of-you thinks he or she is helping you. When annoying statements come from the mouths of other people or when you hear upsetting thoughts in your own mind, take the time to do the Infusion Technique. List all the benefits of being alone.

After you have heard the benefits, send that alone part-of-you to the creative part-of-you to come up with three ways in which you can enjoy the benefits of being alone and you can have a loving relationship. You can learn more about yourself and at the same time learn how you can participate and interact easily with other people who like you. You can feel comfortable and your clothes and hair can be attractive. After you have done the Infusion Technique, you may notice that the negative statements from other people suddenly cease.

CHAPTER 14

Arguments Reveal
Inner Conflict

I have seen the enemy, and it is me.

The Infusion Integration Technique can be used whenever you feel upset, frustrated or angry in your relationships. For instance, when you are experiencing a difference of opinion with another person, stop and ask yourself what does this person represent inside of me? What is the other person really saying? Try to shift your anger before it gets out of control. Do you really have to stick to your point? Would you rather be right than happy? Perhaps you can allow yourself to agree with the other person for the moment. Excuse yourself and breathe some fresh air. Go for a walk, get out of the conflict and think about what is being said. Most people become so involved with being right, they can't hear the other person's point of view.

As you utilize the Infusion Integration Technique more often, you will begin to discover crew members who think they are doing something for you by setting up trauma and drama which create upsetting feelings and events in your life. As you become more aware of the concepts you are holding, you will be able to change your beliefs and shift your relationships.

It is important to understand that you have the power and the strength to change the patterns of your life. You can recognize the slightest discomfort inside of you and know when you are acting in a way that makes you unhappy. You can pay attention when you find yourself reacting to people as they talk to you. You are able to witness yourself overreacting to words, events and activities. Whenever you see that you are not living, acting or being the way you would like to be, take the time to sit quietly and ask the sub-personality who is causing the feeling of unrest and upset, "What are you doing for me?"

At first, it may be difficult to see what the upset part-of-you is doing for you. Sometimes the first answers which come to mind are: "Doing for me? Are you kidding? She's not doing anything for me! She's making me feel sad or upset. She's stopping me from doing what I want." These are negative answers. They are not the answers to the questions: "What are you doing *for* me? What are the advantages of this event, experience or problem?" Allow yourself to relax and look more closely.

As an example, remember a time when you were in an argument with someone. The theory is if you argue or disagree with anyone in your life, it means you have that argument and disagreement happening inside of you. The concept behind this theory is when you experience an argument with someone, it is an outward manifestation of two points of view which are held inside of you.

The point of view which you have not been acknowledging shows up outside of you as an opposite point of view voiced by another person. A person in your life acts out the role of your opposing idea or concept. They will demonstrate the position to show you a hidden belief you hold. You may not consciously think that you are holding a strong belief which matches the other person. You may argue vehemently that you do not think the same way.

Yet an opposite point of view has emerged into your daily life to show you that a disagreement inside of you is important to acknowledge. Yes, it is strange to experience, but when you no longer have arguments inside of you, there are rarely arguments outside of you. I have lived for weeks and months without arguing or disagreeing with the people around me. This has happened often enough for me to know that you can truly release the arguments in your life.

Let us imagine a typical reason for you to engage in an argument or disagreement—someone wants you to do something that you don't want to do. You tell them you don't want to do it. They insist. If they have any authority over you, such as a parent or boss, you may have to do what they say. But if they are equal to you, such as a sibling, co-worker, husband or wife, you may argue with them until one or the other of you gives up, or you may fight to the bitter end, leaving hurt, sorrow, anger or divorce in your wake.

It is important to realize you have a choice. You can choose not to fight and not to disagree. To make a choice of being peaceful requires awareness. You must be aware of your feelings. Observe your feelings about every activity outside of yourself as if you were watching a movie or a play on a stage. When you first start to feel agitated by what someone is saying or doing, do not react to the statement or action as if it were so real or serious. You can stop the action in your movie by changing the scene. You can excuse yourself and go for a walk. You can allow the person who is causing the upset to continue explaining their problem without making it your problem. You have many options and choices in addition to engaging full-heartedly in a heated debate.

The ability to observe the action in your life, rather than always falling prey to your random thoughts and emotions, can be learned and practiced. It can be easier than you think to take control of your life if you will take responsibility for what you are thinking and feeling. If you start paying attention to the connection between the events happening outside of you and the thoughts and beliefs taking place inside of you, you will begin to see that all outside activity is simply a movie production created for your benefit. Perhaps you will decide to create a life which is less dramatic. You might want to change your life into a light comedy, rather than live it as a tragedy.

It is true that the arguments, confusion and conflict which arise in relationships often provide a tremendous opportunity for personal growth. Nevertheless, remember you have the right to choose a partner with whom your growth can be fun and enjoyable. Even if you were to fall in love with someone who is an alcoholic or abusive (usually in these situations, you are in love with their potential), you do not need to commit your life to this person in order to learn to be compassionate and patient. You do not need to be their savior. They need to take responsibility for their own life and seek the help they need to change.

I have found it is not a very good idea to build a relationship based on the interaction found between counselor and patient. This type of relationship often results in the counselor becoming exhausted and depressed because he or she finally realizes that the person they love is not going to change. It is important to remember we can only change ourselves. Our loved ones must want to change and must commit themselves to the inner work necessary to do so. It is healthy to have your limits and set your boundaries.

Almost everyone's life is full of a variety of relationships that can provide personal growth. Your personal love relationship does not have to be abrasive and combative for you to become a better, stronger person. Let yourself choose a love relationship that will be as supportive and as harmonious as possible. You have the right to create a beautiful life. If your partner is incapable of making the necessary changes and continues to create problems for you, perhaps his or her growth will be better served in another environment. Perhaps you have completed that phase of your own growth. Maybe you are ready to let someone provide you with the love and caring that you deserve.

A short analogy might be helpful: Imagine you are climbing a mountain. Your friends and family are with you and some of the people in your party decide to stop and look at the view. You are full of energy and want to keep climbing. You don't feel like stopping. You want to keep going, learning and growing. Bid your friends and loved ones a fond farewell and continue your journey. Don't be sad, you will meet again at the top.

Even in life's smaller dramas, we have the opportunity for personal growth. Imagine for a moment you are being drawn into an argument. Someone wants you to do something you don't want to do. They keep insisting and you keep resisting. An example: you are asked to wash the windows at your home. Friends will be visiting, and your mother, wife, a friend, whoever insists you must stay home and wash the windows.

You want to go shopping. The visitors will be staying for several days, and you would like this opportunity to go out for a while. Besides, you truly dislike washing windows. The streaks never seem to come off, and the person who wants the windows clean is never satisfied with your results.

This example seems very straightforward, and this may seem to be a silly reason to engage in an argument. Yet I am certain that you can remember even sillier examples of reasons you have argued with someone. The discussion goes something like this:

Other Person: "Where are you going?"

You: "Shopping."

Other Person: "Shopping? How can you go shopping at a time like this? You know that our friends will be here any minute."

You: "They won't be here for a couple of hours, and I want to go shopping."

Other Person: "Are you blind? Can't you see the windows need washing? There's so much to do. You don't care about me."

You: "What's that got to do with it? They're your friends anyway. You just don't understand me!"

Notice the lack of direct communication in this discussion. The personal attacks which create hurt and bitterness are thrown into a conversation about washing windows and going shopping. It would appear that these two people have had many arguments and disagreements. They can barely communicate without creating confusion and frustration.

Handling an argument is tricky. Even after years of using the Infusion Integration Technique, I often have to pause and think carefully about how every event outside of me is a reflection of what is being thought about inside of me. It is so very easy to deny that the other person in this story has anything to do with me. She is obviously mean, terrible and doesn't listen. She is just in my life to bother me. She cannot be a part-of-me!

Wrong. If the theory is consistent, then every person in my life represents a part-of-me, like it or not. Therefore, we must ask, "What is this window washing fanatic doing for me?"

I separate the two parts by asking them to be represented by my hands. The one who wants me to wash windows and the one who wants to go shopping will each talk.

Think carefully with me. What is this window fanatic trying to accomplish by having me stay home and wash windows? Move into the point of view of this person who is insisting I stay home and work, rather than go out and play.

The window fanatic says: "I want my home to look clean and well-managed. I want to be responsible and take care of my duties so I will feel proud of my environment when company comes to visit. I feel that my home and friends are important. My belief is that everything in my environment needs to be perfectly arranged and clean, especially when company is coming."

The part who wants to forget about the visitors and wants to run away from the window washing and go shopping says: "I want to have fun. I don't want to wash windows. Our visitors won't notice the windows anyway. I didn't notice they were dirty. Why should they? My belief is I should be able to do what I want to do, when I want to do it!"

I now ask the shopper, "What if there were a way you could have fun washing the windows and go shopping? Would you be willing to change your behavior and clean the windows?"

I have chosen to settle this argument by accomplishing both needs expressed. The part who wants everything to look perfect could possibly be persuaded to change her mind and forget the window washing or perhaps I can accomplish both.

The shopper answers: "Have fun washing the windows? Are you crazy?"

"Just consider the idea. What if washing windows could be fun? You could do it easily and quickly and have time to go shopping. If it were possible, would you be willing to change your behavior and wash the windows and satisfy the person who wants it done, and also go shopping?"

"Well, I suppose if window washing could be fun (which I doubt) and I still had time to go shopping and if I could get this 'maniac' off my back, I might do it."

"Good. Now I'd like to ask the window fanatic: What if the windows were washed and they didn't have to be perfect and you still had time to enjoy yourself and go shopping and do things you'd like to do?"

The window fanatic answers: "I want everything to be perfect. My home reflects me. I know I'm not perfect; that's why I work so hard."

"I understand, but what if everything didn't have to be perfect? Perfection implies an end result, a completion. If you look at the universe, at nature, you will notice that it is not in a state of completion, but in a state of creation. Creation is not perfect, but is always evolving and changing. If you were perfect you would be an angel in heaven. So being perfect may not be the most appropriate way to proceed on your journey called life. Therefore, if you could experience a sense of satisfaction in what you have accomplished, and you were willing not to be perfect, then you would have more time to enjoy yourself, to go shopping and relax. Would you be willing to change your behavior if you could feel a sense of accomplishment?"

"Well, I guess that makes sense," the window fanatic answers. "Being perfect seems impossible, but experiencing a sense of accomplishment might be doable. Yes, I am willing to try this new behavior."

"Good. I would now like the window fanatic and the shopper to go to the creative part-of-me and come up with at least three ways to do the following: have fun washing windows, easily and quickly, and allow time to go shopping. You don't need to be perfect, but instead can experience a sense of accomplishment about what you have done, and you can have time to enjoy yourself and relax."

I ask all parts-of-me to check those three ways and make certain the solutions are a win-win situation for all parts-of-me. Now I hold my hands two feet apart and slowly bring them together until the palms are touching and bring them to my chest. I see the two parts, the window fanatic and the shopper looking at each other and then hugging each other, realizing they are one person. I see all parts-of-me forming a huddle around the two in the center, directing love to them. I feel my Higher Self hovering overhead, sending love to the two opponents and out to all parts-of-me.

I see the two walking hand in hand, sharing concepts and ideas. They realize each made their decisions based on information available to them in the past. They can now be open to new creative solutions which will allow them to feel a sense of accomplishment and also have time to relax and have fun. We thank you for sharing in consciousness.

You may notice that many of the same words are used in the Infusion Integration Technique. Once you have learned the basic process, it is similar to singing a well-remembered song. By using a similar pattern to integrate the different parts-of-you, it is easy to quickly accomplish the Infusion process. The primary challenge is to determine what the part-of-you who is creating the problem is doing *for* you. This awareness requires allowing the mind to search for the advantages of what may seem to be totally non-beneficial events and activities.

CHAPTER 15

Mastering
Impatience

Business Time Versus "Real" Time

One of my frustrations in the business world has been to watch people in the corporate environment become very bureaucratic and slow in accomplishing their goals. There is a part-of-me who becomes upset if I have been waiting for a contract to be signed or an order to be placed, and I learn it will be months before the people in charge will be able to perform their part of the negotiations. When someone tells me it will be six months, maybe nine months, before something can happen, I begin to lose my mind. Emotions rise to the surface that are not pleasant to behold. I'm sure some of you know what I mean, especially when your livelihood depends upon these types of decisions.

Waiting for any experience can be frustrating because we so often live our lives in the future. We make plans and rehearse those planned events in our minds until they seem totally real. Many of us live a future event over and over in our minds. The future event may seem more important to us than anything that is happening during a typical day of our current lives.

Living in the future can be dangerous because we are preventing ourselves from experiencing this moment. When we are daydreaming about tomorrow, next week, or next year, we are focusing on an illusion we have created. We are not paying attention to our lives now.

Unfortunately, we are often not satisfied with the actual event we have so carefully planned when it finally happens. It doesn't always happen the way we've been rehearsing it. People at the event don't always deliver the lines we had hoped they would say. Their actions may be different than what we had hoped for. We become disappointed, upset, sad and angry. Our frustration moves our minds, again, out of the present and we scurry off to another planned future event, watching it unfold in our imagination.

Planning for the future and being aware of our preferences can be delightful. Living in the future and concentrating on our goals to the exclusion of being in the present can undermine our ability to change, create, grow and develop as human beings. Our point of power is in the present moment. It has been called the holy instant because, if you are completely present, you have the power of the universe flowing through you.

The following exercise may help to change your pattern of impatience and frustration. Separate the two parts-of-you who have opinions about patience. Ask the part who becomes impatient to be represented by one hand. Ask your patient part, the one who understands that delays are simply the way of business or life, to be represented by the other hand. We will ask these two to express their points of view.

Ask the impatient part: "What are you doing *for* me by being impatient? What are the advantages of being upset when you learn it will be months before a contract is signed? What is your underlying belief?" The impatient part answers: "I'm keeping you on your toes. You've got to follow up and push your clients to make things happen. You need a lot of customers and different deals pending so you can have a good income. My belief is that you can't trust the corporate environment, therefore, you have to be on guard at all times."

The patient part-of-me speaks: "I believe we can plan for the future, but our present moment is more important than any future moment. We cannot live in the future, therefore, we must live joyfully today. If we become upset when there is a delay, we are wasting the moment in confusion. We need to use our time constructively. If our head is clear, we may discover a more creative way to accomplish our goals. I believe it is important to live peacefully. Nothing is worth becoming upset about. We can feel sad and disappointed, but we don't have to ruin our days by living in a state of frustration."

The impatient part responds: "She's a nut. How can you live like that? It's impossible."

"I understand what you're saying, but maybe she has a point. Maybe there is a way you can work together to make things happen rather than fight each other all the time. Maybe the patient and impatient parts-of-me can find a way to create a consensus.

"I'd now like to ask the impatient part: If there were a way I could be alert and aware, I could receive a good income and trust the corporate world, would you be willing to change your behavior and let me relax even if there's a delay in a contract or order?"

"Maybe."

"Good. I'll accept maybe and I will close my eyes and go to the creative part-of-me to ask for three ways I can be alert, aware and receive a good income. I can trust people in the business world. I can relax and live joyfully. I will use my time constructively and live peacefully and patiently. I now ask all parts-of-me to check those three ways and make sure they are win-win solutions. I don't need to know what those three ways are in consciousness at this time."

I hold my hands two feet apart in front of me with the palms facing each other. Slowly, the two parts-of-me move toward each other as my hands come together until the palms are touching, and I bring them to my heart.

The patient and impatient part-of-me hug each other and blend together until they are one. I realize the impatient part was simply acting out feelings based on limited information gathered long ago. New, more complete information is now flooding this impatient part as she begins to realize that there is no longer a need to overreact when events are delayed.

All parts-of-me form a huddle around the two in the center, directing love to them. My Higher Self sends love down through the two in the center and out to all parts-of-me. The two walk hand in hand, sharing concepts and ideas as I begin to see that I no longer need to battle with life. I can live peacefully, even when I am doing business. I will begin to act differently and events will be seen in a new way. I am available for all parts-of-me to discuss their feelings and ideas. I thank these two for sharing in consciousness at this time.

I will rest in the knowledge that I can live more patiently, seeing life as an unfoldment, being able to rest and relax in the flow. I will take time to breathe deeply. I will be aware of each step when I am walking. I will observe my environment and notice the changes in the sky as the sun makes its way from horizon to horizon. I will not need to hurry this life along, but will notice how it offers many surprises and interesting twists and turns to be witnessed and enjoyed. I will value each moment, rather than worry about creating a better moment, when I am richer, thinner, prettier, more loved, more successful, etc. Each moment my experience creates who I am, so I will remain present to watch my baby steps, my walking briskly, my running, laughing, playing, working, all of it, in the here and now, in this eternal moment.

CHAPTER 16

Are You Ready for Perfect Health?

The four cornerstones of life are
health, wealth, love and self-expression.
Without health our foundation begins to tilt.

The body is a magnificent creation. It is an incredible expression of consciousness. Billions of cells reproduce and work together to efficiently serve the host, which is you. Without thinking about the mechanism, you are able to digest your food, your heart beats, your blood circulates, your lungs breathe. Millions of complex interactions take place inside of you to support your life every second of the day.

Yet, on occasion, you may find the body's superb functioning is unable to perform efficiently. You might not digest your food easily, a headache may develop and you may suffer from a cold or the flu. Germs and viruses seem to infiltrate your system, and disease becomes your primary focus until you are well again. You may experience being overweight or being too thin. Your skin breaks out or you become allergic to foods or environmental influences.

Through my own life experience I know the effects of disease. I experienced all the childhood illnesses—measles, mumps and chicken pox—in the extreme. I seemed to have a tendency toward bronchitis and spent many winter months trying to recuperate from bouts of near pneumonia. As a teenager and young adult, I was overweight, and my skin was constantly breaking out. I had intense headaches, and the muscles in my neck and back seemed to always be tight and aching.

After becoming an adult, I began studying medical books and alternative methods of healing. I learned medicine often seemed to help the body to recover, but drugs alone seemed to have a limited effect on curing disease and problems in the body. I really wanted to know how to prevent illness and how to rebound quickly if I started to become ill.

One of the first breakthroughs in awareness for me was the study of "Touch for Health," a technique which explained how to change the energy in the body and help the healing process by massaging certain lymph glands, touching acupressure points and realigning meridians of energy in the body. This information was gleaned from Chinese medicine, which has utilized these theories to heal diseases for thousands of years. It seemed as if I had discovered a missing link in the care and maintenance of the body. I felt as if I had been given a body without the owner's manual, and I was finally able to understand how blockages of energy affected different body parts.

I found that the Infusion Integration Technique could take me a step further in helping me understand why I had created an illness, or even an accident, in my life. I looked closely at the possibility that every event, experience and illness might be created by a part-of-me who thought it was doing something *for* me. I began to discover that my diseases and accidents have been powerful tools to force me to stop, look and listen to what a part-of-me was trying to communicate.

I have learned that nearly every illness and disorder in the body seems to be correlated with powerful, positive reasons for creating the experience. It is interesting to note that the people with whom I have used the Infusion Integration Technique usually seem to know why they have created the problem. They usually have an answer to the question: "What is this illness or problem doing *for* me?" Of course, they frequently begin to answer by saying: "It's not doing anything for me. It's making me miserable!" But if you continue questioning yourself or others, you may soon find the reasons for the problem.

WHAT ABOUT WEIGHT PROBLEMS?

Being overweight may seem to be simply the result of overeating and doing very little exercise. Yet I have noticed that many people who are not overweight eat whatever they want and exercise intermittently. What is the difference? I believe there is a part-of-us who believes it is doing something *for* us by creating a weight problem. When I looked within me, I found some of the beliefs the overweight part-of-me was holding:

- I could eat whatever I wanted.
- I didn't have to be disciplined.
- The fat protected me from male aggression.
- Men didn't try to rape me.
- Being fat made it easier to have female and male friends.
- I didn't have to be the center of attention.
- People paid attention to my mind rather than my body.
- If I fell down, the padding on my thighs and hips
  protected me from breaking my bones.
- Extra weight kept me feeling strong and healthy.
- Fat made me look better because it filled out my face and chest.

The underlying belief I held was that being overweight was a form of protection. Isn't it amazing what the mind can fabricate? All those reasons worked very well; and no matter which diets I tried, I always gained back what little weight I had lost. The overweight part-of-me considered it dangerous to be slender.

Finally, I did the Infusion Integration Technique. I asked the overweight part-of-me: "What if I could have all the advantages of being overweight and could wear a size 10 dress? Would you be willing to change your behavior and let me release the weight I no longer need on my body?" (The entire process is described in Chapter 12.)

It worked. I now wear a size 8-10 outfit and feel comfortable in my curvy new figure. I do eat what I want, but I no longer have a desire to eat a lot of sweets, dairy or fats. I don't eat any meat, just a slice of fish maybe once a week. I can still finish off five oatmeal cookies with a glass of skim milk in about two minutes, eat a bowl of frozen yogurt or maybe a special dessert after a great pasta dinner. But it's interesting to note that I no longer have a desire to eat very much at any one time. A bowl of cereal and fruit in the morning will hold me until a late lunch, when I may have an avocado, tomato and lettuce sandwich or fruit and cottage cheese. Dinner is usually vegetables with pasta or rice, and maybe a salad.

I work in the garden and walk in the hills around my house, but not every day. I do not have a disciplined program of exercise. And my weight stays the same. I believe it is because the overweight part-of-me now knows I am protected and safe without being fat.

COLDS AND THE FLU

In my new lifestyle, illness seems to be a thing of the past. The same number of germs still reside in my throat and nasal passages, but I don't seem to catch a cold or the flu very often. Why not? I no longer need to be sick to give myself an excuse to rest and relax. I am not suggesting that you want to be sick with a cold, flu or some other disease. I am proposing that maybe a part-of-you believes it is doing something for you by creating the illness to stop you, to let you relax, to give you a break.

As I was learning how my thoughts create my reality, I had an extraordinary revelation during a rain-soaked day on the Monterey Peninsula. I had just finished a day of work and walked out into the rain to go to my car in the parking lot. In about three minutes time I was at the car door, and I suddenly realized that my throat was sore. In less than three minutes in the rain, I had changed from feeling healthy to experiencing an intense soreness in my throat.

"This is incomprehensible. It's ridiculous!" I said to myself. "How could I develop a sore throat so quickly?"

Then my mother's words echoed through the years: "Don't go out in the rain without an umbrella, you'll get a sore throat." I had committed the ultimate crime. I had walked out in the rain without an umbrella. My head was exposed to the rain. Thus, of course, I developed a sore throat.

Needless to say, I asked the sore throat part-of-me what she was doing for me by creating the sore throat, especially so quickly. The answer: to prove Mother was right. Rain creates a sore throat, which leads to a cold, then bronchitis and the flu. Besides, you're tired, you need to rest. You won't relax unless you get sick, so this is the beginning of your time of relaxation.

I then asked: "What if there were a way I could walk with rain beating on my head and soaking me thoroughly, and I wouldn't get a sore throat or the flu, and I could still respect my mother? What if I would take the time to relax and rest? I won't go out tonight. I'll go to bed early. Would you be willing to change your behavior and let me be healthy?" The answer was yes. We did the Infusion Technique. The sore throat went away as quickly as it had appeared. I no longer seem to develop sore throats, colds or the flu.

LIFE-THREATENING ILLNESS

Many times I have worked with people who were experiencing life-threatening illnesses. When I ask what the illness is doing for them, they usually know why they created the disease. Often, when they are facing death, the part which created the illness believes death is the only way out of their upsetting lives.

No, the total person does not want to die, but one part has decided the only way out is death. This part may be trying to escape a miserable job, marriage, debt, overwhelming loss, any number of circumstances, and they feel there is no other way out. Using the Infusion Integration Technique can help this confused sub-personality, who is determined to die, to realize there may be other options. By opening communications with the creative part-of-their-being, they can discover more creative ways to change their life.

I was surprised to see the positive change in an eighteen-year-old girl who worked with me at the Pebble Beach resort. She had developed cancer in her leg. I decided to go out on a limb and see if I could help her with the Infusion Technique. I asked if she would be willing to play a game with me to see if I could help her with the cancer. After thinking about it for a moment, she agreed. (At the time, I felt I was perhaps being too bold to propose the process, but I also thought we had nothing to lose by trying.)

I asked her to separate the two parts-of-herself: the one who had created the cancer and the one who was fighting the disease. She glared at the hand which was supposed to represent the cancer creating part-of-her. I then asked what this part was doing for her. She immediately said it was doing nothing for her, just making her scared and sick.

I then said, "Well, this is a life-threatening disease. Did something happen to you which made you want to die?"

She immediately said yes. She had been raped at age fourteen and for years she had been deeply depressed and wanted to die.

I then asked the part-of-her who wanted to live, "What do you think about having cancer and dying?"

The part who wanted to live said, "I understand how the cancer creating part-of-me felt, but I feel so much better now about life. I have a boyfriend and a job, and I want to live."

I asked the part who had wanted to die if she were able to let the feelings of the rape fade away? Could she allow herself to feel the love from her boyfriend and realize she has a good life ahead of her? Would she be willing to let this girl become well and live a long and happy life?

The part-of-her which had created the cancer agreed to try. We did the Infusion Technique. The last I heard, she is in remission and is happy with her family and friends.

Another example of a major illness being changed was a friend who had a tumor on her ovary. She was scheduled for an operation the next week. I suggested that we do the Infusion Technique, just to see if anything might happen. I asked the tumor creating part-of-her what it was doing for her by creating this tumor. She answered that it wasn't doing anything for her except causing her pain.

I had heard tumors are often created through an energy blockage established five to ten years earlier after a shocking event. I asked her if she had gone through a difficult event five to ten years ago. She immediately responded affirmatively.

Her daughter had been in a terrible accident eight years earlier. The mother had prayed for her own life to be taken to spare her daughter's life. I asked the woman if her daughter had survived. She said yes. The girl was alive and doing fine.

I said, "Well, then, you no longer need to keep the oath of dying for your daughter. She's alive and so are you."

We did the Infusion Technique, sending the part-of-her who had created the tumor to the creative part-of-her. I asked both parts to discover three ways in which she could be perfectly healthy and would not need to have the tumor or die to keep her daughter well. When she went for x-rays the week before surgery, the tumor was gone.

Do I suggest you avoid surgery? No, definitely not. I do encourage you to look for the underlying beliefs and possible reasons for an illness or accident. But often the true understanding and healing does not occur until after you have removed the problem from your body, if this is possible.

In 1982, I learned firsthand what it means to say, "Yes, I will go in for surgery." I had developed a very painful case of endometriosis with tumors on my ovaries. The creeping crud, as I called it, covered my reproductive organs and intestines. I tried many different techniques, even psychic healing, which helped to relieve the pain, but I could not erase the damage. So I went in for surgery. The removal of the tumors and scar tissue was a tremendous relief. Immediately after surgery, the pain was gone.

Using the Infusion Technique, I was able to see what the crud and the pain had been doing *for* me. The part-of-me which had created the endometriosis had been trying to let me know that I was denying my femininity. I was living the life of a macho lady, working as an executive in the business world, and trying to control everything in my life. Even up to and after surgery, I continued this life pattern until 1987. I was very stubborn. Therefore, it was efficient and helpful to clean out my painful endometriosis surgically. Eventually, I hoped to understand the reason for my difficult experience.

The changes in behavior brought about by the Infusion Technique don't necessarily work to heal people in the ways we want it to. Yet I have found Infusion to be extremely effective in helping the body, mind and spirit to come to agreement. The Infusion Integration Technique helps you to understand the reasons behind an experience, an illness, an accident or an event.

The Infusion Technique may help a seriously ill person to become peaceful and relaxed. The family can give love and support as the individual lives in peace and with dignity until they are ready to move from this life.

Dying is a part of life, and to say we have failed in some way because we die is to deny that in this finite world there is a beginning and an end to this particular incarnation. Whether we go on to heaven, other lifetimes, other dimensions or merge with the universe, there is a time to go; and it is often the responsibility of family and friends to help the person, as much as possible, make an easy and dignified transition with a minimum of fear and tribulation.

I had one fascinating experience helping a man whose heart was barely working. He had lived through several surgeries. Yet the doctors had told him there was nothing more they could do. He had a very short time left to live. It could be days or weeks. The son knew his father did not want to leave the family and was fighting to stay alive. The grand old man was still able to walk on a Tuesday when I saw him at his son's home. He and his family were from India. They were very sweet and caring people.

We met in an all white living room. Everything was white: the carpet, walls, curtains and furniture. The only color was in several beautiful pastel and gold paintings. The elderly, slender man with white hair came into the room. We talked for a few minutes about the lovely day, and then I suggested we try the Infusion Technique. When I asked the part-of-him who had created the heart problems what he was doing for this man, he replied, "Life is a struggle, and I must fight my way through it." He raised his arms and clenched his fists to demonstrate the feeling of the battle he had experienced all his life.

I could see the tension in his hands, arms, chest and face, which I knew were a reflection of the emotional battle this man had fought within. It was easy to imagine this chronic state of stress possibly being a significant factor in the development of his heart disease.

I asked, "If there were a way you could change your feeling, and no longer felt you needed to fight, would you be willing to end the battle?" He agreed to try. We went through the Infusion Technique and sent the fighting part-of-him to the creative part-of-him to discover ways he could release himself from the battle.

When I called two days later, the son told me his father had changed dramatically after we had completed the Infusion Integration Technique. He was happy and light-hearted and seemed to be feeling better. The next day I called again, and learned that his father had died quietly in his sleep. I felt very sad. I began to give my condolences.

The son stopped me and said, "No, I don't think you understand. The last few days of my father's life were the first time I saw him in a truly peaceful state. It brought me tremendous joy to see him finally happy. Perhaps he has taken this new feeling of peace with him." Then I began to understand. This man had completely released himself from the battle, and now he was free.

WHAT ABOUT ACCIDENTS?

For many years, my specialty in creating disorder and chaos in my life was to experience accidents. I was called accident-prone by my family, friends and a local newspaper. One of my major accidents was cutting my feet in a lawn mower when I was twelve years old. I lost my little toe and cut all the tendons on the top of my left foot. This required skin-grafting from my thighs, which left unattractive scars. I was in and out of the hospital for two months and unable to walk for over a year. After I learned to walk again, I fell down often, especially going downstairs. Later, I realized the falls were the result of my refusal to pay attention to my feet and legs. I had disowned them.

I had many car accidents. People would rear-end me in traffic on the freeway and slam into the side of my car at intersections. I seemed to be a disaster looking for a place to happen.

Then the next major accident happened when I was twenty-seven. I was stabbed in the back by an assailant in a parking garage. My lung collapsed, and I went into a period of extreme fear.

Finally, in 1990, I fell down the steps in a movie theater and broke my foot and rib. Two weeks later, I fell off the crutches and cracked my spine. I was in bed for five months and experienced tremendous losses, including my business, my relationship, my home and self-confidence. I was very sad and extremely depressed.

What I gained in my final major accident was a deep understanding of why I was accident-prone. I realized, during the many hours of not being able to move, that I must look at this accident problem. I could see my accidents were life-threatening. I could imagine my friends saying, "Isn't it too bad Verlaine was killed in an accident?"

I needed to know the underlying belief causing this constant battering of my body. I realized if anyone were treating me as badly as I was treating myself, I would put them in jail. I saw myself lying in bed, unable to move, and realized I had put myself in a type of jail!

I looked closely at the circumstances leading up to the first accident when I cut my feet in the lawn mower. It was early evening. Dad, my brother and I each had a lawn mower cutting the acre of grass around our home in Iowa. I had been trimming around the edge of our driveway and started moving up the hill. Suddenly, I decided to back up and catch a clump of tall grass.

I turned around and saw that my nine-year-old brother was right behind me trying to keep up with his large, automatic mower. He thought I was going to move forward and there I was right in front of his mower. Dad hadn't put the front guard on the large mower, so first my right foot, then my left foot slid into the whirling blades.

The next thing I remember was laying on the grass, grabbing my feet covered with mangled shoes and socks. I could see the neighbor kids staring down at me. I felt the stump of my little toe on my right foot. My father, mother and Pat Dittmer, a volunteer fireman, bundled me into the car and off to the hospital. Pat was holding me in the back seat. He told me not to worry about my little toe. He was keeping it safe in his pocket. He said the doctors could sew it back on. His assurances gave me little comfort because I was certain there was much more damage than just the little toe.

I was rushed into surgery, and awoke the next morning to see large casts stretching from my thighs down over my feet. As they wheeled me to x-ray, I started crying. The nurse asked me if I was in pain, and I said yes, but I was crying for a different reason. She asked what she could do. I asked, haltingly, between the tears, could she please count my toes? I couldn't see them because the cast was too tall. She counted nine toes, and I cried with relief. I knew the little toe was gone, but I had hoped the doctors would be able to save the other toes.

It was a long tiresome year. I went through skin grafts and additional surgeries. I was confined to a wheelchair. Then after this very trying year, my father left my family.

Mom and Dad had argued and fought as long as I could remember, mostly about Dad being on the road as a traveling salesman. He only came home on the weekends, and Mom really didn't like him being away all week. Rather than making life lovely on the weekends, she would spend much of the time haranguing him for his lifestyle. They had built a lovely home with a beautiful view of the Mississippi River, but the sadness inside the house would reach a crescendo on many weekends.

Thirty-four years later, while lying on my bed with my broken left foot, I realized my foot was now aching in the very same place that had been most injured in the lawn mower accident. There had been no feeling on the top part of my foot since I was twelve years old. In the fall down the stairs, my foot was pulled backwards, breaking the tendons loose from the bones, reawakening the pain of the lawn mower incident. I began to piece together patterns that had developed over time.

Looking back at my childhood, I realized how responsible I had felt for my parents' divorce. I looked closer and closer until I realized maybe, just maybe, a part-of-me had come up with the idea of being in an accident, which might keep my parents together. Perhaps subconsciously I knew they were about to break up. After all, they did stay together an additional year after the accident. At the end of this difficult year, I'll never forget Dad taking the family to a large, beautiful lake for a picnic where we went swimming. Dad and I were sitting alone on the blanket, eating corn on the cob. Mom and my brother were getting something from the car. Dad asked me if I was feeling better. I replied, "Yes, I am definitely recovered." The next day he left a note to mother saying that he was leaving permanently. The drama of this departure could fill another book.

I looked at the possibility that this accident could have been seen by my subconscious mind as a deterrent to my parents breaking up the family. It seemed like a far-fetched idea. Could a part-of-me create an accident to keep my parents together?

Then I looked at the stabbing incident. It was August 1971, and my live-in boyfriend was moving to San Francisco to accept a new job. We were in agreement about the move, and that eventually I would follow. I had taken him to the airport on Sunday. I was stabbed Monday evening. My boyfriend flew home immediately.

I examined closely the fall down the stairs, the broken foot and rib. I realized, once again, before the accident the man in my life was leaving me. After the accident, he stayed longer. There definitely seemed to be a pattern. A part-of-me believed the way to keep the man in my life from leaving me was to have an accident. I asked that part-of-me what it was doing *for* me, and the major answer was: I am helping you to keep the man in your life from leaving. Besides the only time I allow myself to receive and relax is when I am hurt. Otherwise, I am giving to others around me all the time.

I asked the accident-prone part-of-me who had created accidents *for* me, "If there were a way that I could be a receiving, relaxed person, and if the man in my life wanted to be with me, and I didn't need to have an accident to keep him with me, would that part be willing to change her behavior and let me be accident-free?" She agreed. We did the Infusion Technique, and I have been accident-free since 1990.

The issues around accidents and illness can be very difficult to penetrate because we are often so invested in the underlying belief which perpetuates the problem. It took me a long time to understand my pattern. Even though the first accident didn't keep my father from leaving my family, my accident-prone sub-personality continued her behavior. I seemed to have an accident whenever I was faced with the departure of a man I cared about. This part-of-me was caught in the idea of accidents as solutions, until I was able to recognize and change the pattern.

As you may notice, the idea in this game of Infusion is not to judge the sub-personality who has made the decision to create accidents, illnesses and problems. The idea is to understand, beyond a shadow of a doubt, that this part-of-you who is creating the problem thinks it is doing something *for* you, even though the solution may seem ridiculous or even dangerous. The challenge is to change the behavior of this sub-personality by recognizing what it is trying to accomplish, then send that part to the creative part-of-you to discover new ways to accomplish the same goals in a win-win manner.

ABUSIVE RELATIONSHIPS

Fortunately, not everyone is experiencing abusive relationships. But if you are, it is imperative you utilize these same techniques to free yourself from abusive patterns. When I experienced my accidents, I felt in many ways as if I were a battered woman; but I was the one doing the battering. If we continue our theory, then everyone outside of ourselves is a representative of a part-of-us. The people who abuse others are representing an energy on the outside that the abused person is feeling on the inside. This statement in no way condones the behavior of the assailant. They are often terribly dangerous and should not share a household with anyone until they confront and resolve their own issues and deal with their anger and fear.

Yet the reason for bringing up this issue is because many people, usually women, are victims of this type of abuse and need to release themselves from these relationships. Using the language of the Infusion Technique: "What possibly could this abusive part-of-you be doing for you?"

The first response might be, "Making me feel worthless, unloved, unwanted." But these statements are the negative responses. They don't describe what the beatings or torment are doing *for* you.

I know this sounds ridiculous to say that someone hurting you is doing something for you, but try to see a pattern. Look closely at the terrible beliefs. In what way could you possibly be benefiting from this horrible behavior?

Possible underlying beliefs are that relationships are violent, and people become violent when they are troubled, when they drink and when they take drugs.

A belief may become your truth, and the universe may prove it to you. So if you change your belief, you may change your truth, and thus your reality. For example, rather than believing that all relationships are abusive, you can change your belief to some relationships are joyful and peaceful, which is also true.

What is the abusive part-of-you doing *for* you? Possible answers include the following:

- Abuse makes me strong and resilient.
- Abuse lets me know I can take anything and bounce back.
- Abuse keeps me on guard and aware of my environment.
- Abuse makes me pay close attention to my behavior.
- Abuse teaches me to pay attention to details.
- Abuse gives me a dramatic, non-boring life.
- Abuse keeps me humble.
- Abuse keeps me from becoming lazy.
- Abuse gives me the punishment I think I deserve.
- Abuse makes me find a way to help change my abuser.
- Abuse is part of life and no one else will ever care about me.

Try to think of other ways abuse may be doing something *for* you. Even if you have never been physically battered, you may have felt attacked emotionally or mentally.

Think about what your abusive sub-personality might be trying to accomplish by creating this experience. Make a list of reasons. Then ask the abusive part-of-you: "If there were a way I could be strong and resilient and all my reasons for experiencing abuse could be met in a positive way, would you be willing to let me live a peaceful, loving life?"

When the answer is yes, send the abusive part-of-you to the creative part-of-you to find three ways in which:

- You can be strong and resilient.
- You can learn how to live life in a positive way and bounce back from any negative events.
- You'll be very aware of your environment.
- You will pay close attention to details and live an interesting, non-boring life without being abused.
- You can stay humble and not be lazy.
- You no longer need to feel you deserve to be punished.
- You don't have to be abused physically, emotionally or mentally for the rest of your life.

Continue with the rest of the Infusion Technique as described in Chapter 12. (You may have the entire process memorized by now.) You will see yourself behaving in new ways. The aggressor in your life may change his or her behavior, or he or she may no longer be in your life. When you have changed your core beliefs, there is less danger of again finding yourself in a similar relationship. If, by chance, this procedure does not give you the courage to leave or change, go through it again, looking closely at the underlying beliefs and your reasons for experiencing these difficult circumstances. You may need to seek the guidance of a professional counselor to assist you in making these necessary, but often difficult, changes in your life.

Creating perfect health is an ongoing process. Looking at the reasons for manifesting a headache, a backache or any other type of disorder will help you to become more aware of what you are feeling and thinking. You will begin to understand how your thoughts and emotions are affecting your physical body.

At the same time, it is possible to discover how the physical properties of food and the environment may also be influencing your health. It is true that you can learn to overcome the ramifications of various allergies or reactions to food and environmental pollutants. It does help to be cognizant of your current weaknesses, so you can overcome the resistance to these often subtle forms of health disturbances.

Health and well-being are vital for all activities, yet we often take it for granted that health will always be ours. Since I have had to face health problems, I have become interested in a variety of methods to create health and well-being. I have found it is possible to incorporate and utilize all the various points of view including western medicine, eastern traditions, alternative methods of healing, and the Infusion Integration Technique to maintain a vibrant and healthy body.

CHAPTER 17

You Are Your Self-Expression

I'm healthy, wealthy, and in love,
but something's missing. What could it be?
Your ability to express creatively!

Each of us is born with a boundless supply of creative energy. And throughout our lives we have the opportunity to utilize this creativity in a variety of ways. In reality, the most profound creative experience is the living of life. Our lives are indeed our greatest work of art. I have heard it said that one of the purposes of our life on earth is to learn how to create through form. If you think about the tremendous number of objects of every description made by man (the inventions, the practical tools and equipment, the objects of art and design, the music, clothing, automobiles—the list is endless and ever-growing), it is truly awesome to realize the enormous amount of creativity we are displaying.

Yet in this information age of comfort and convenience, many people are not expressing their creativity. They are doing paperwork in an office or doing some mundane task, which helps to pay the bills, but does not fulfill their need to create. I believe this loss of direct creative experience often results in the feeling of emptiness and worthlessness that some individuals are experiencing, even if they are successful according to worldly standards. They may be making money. They're healthy and perhaps they have love in their lives. Yet it feels as if something is missing. Of course, many people do not have wealth, health or the love they need. Thus, they may feel the foundation of their lives is rather shaky.

When I visited the island of Bali, in Indonesia, I was surprised to learn that they do not have a word for art. The reason they don't have such a word is because everyone is an artist. Each day the villagers work in the rice fields and prepare food for their families, and they all create paintings or carvings, sew, dye fabrics, prepare delicate flower and fruit offerings to honor nature, etc. They all work with their creativity every day. The smiling, relaxed faces seem to reflect the inner peace one feels when you are among the Balinese. I am certain they have their own problems, but much of the tension and concerns we see in our western societies do not seem to be reflected in these people.

What I am suggesting is your artist and communications sub-personalities may be aching to express themselves creatively in the world. Within you may be the artist, musician, dancer, writer of poetry or prose, the speaker, storyteller, filmmaker, designer, potter, sculptor or gardener who when able to express themselves will let your heart sing and help your soul release its storehouse of abundant treasures.

Seven years ago, when I was in the midst of acting as corporate vice president of a high technology company, I felt exhausted, wasted, ancient and unfulfilled. I was making a huge salary plus commissions and was part owner of the company. According to society's dictates, I should have felt proud and excited about my life. Instead, each day was drudgery, and I could hardly wait for it to end. What was wrong with this picture? The work was not creative for me. The very same job could be very creative for someone else, but it was not a stimulus for my creative energy. It was not fulfilling for me.

I have found it is important to learn what you enjoy doing, and, as much as possible, use your enjoyment of a project or activity as your criteria for a career. I have always enjoyed writing. It is easy for me, and I love to watch the words flow out about various subjects and ideas. At one point in my life, I decided to apply for a job at a newspaper, and luck was with me. I was hired as editor of six weekly papers. The truth was my getting the job was not luck. I had consciously decided what I wanted, I had written my list, and my intuition led me to the small town newspaper on the exact day the editor had quit. Another time, I was working in the traffic department of an advertising agency. I wanted very much to be a copywriter for the agency but didn't think I could have such a position (since I did not have the proper degrees from a university). I talked to the head copywriter over lunch one day, and he revealed to me that he also had not graduated from college. He said the most important ingredient for success as a writer was the ability and desire to write, not a college degree. He read my writings and encouraged me to continue. Soon I was chief copywriter for a top ad agency on Wilshire Boulevard in Los Angeles. It was very exciting working with the creative director and writing copy for radio, television, magazines and brochures.

You can use your creative spark wherever you are now, and you can allow yourself to open up to the possibility of letting your dreams become reality. A couple, who were friends of mine, had found they enjoyed making decorative candles. They started out very simply, just making a few candles for friends at Christmas time. Because the candles were so lovely, soon people were asking if they could buy candles from them to give as gifts. They started taking orders. Gift shop owners in their small town saw the candles and asked to order them. They were encouraged to take a variety of the candles to the large gift show in a nearby city and soon had orders from all over the country. They were in business. Their hobby, their creative expression of love, had become their livelihood.

Another lady friend decided to decorate a large basket she had bought in Mexico as a bassinet and carrier for her small baby. She covered it in a delightful fabric and trimmed it with lace. Everywhere she went people asked where she had found such a great baby basket. She told them she had made it. They wanted to buy such a basket. She took orders. Soon she was in business with national distribution.

I could go on and on with stories about people who started a hobby, a creative expression they enjoyed, and made it into a way of life. In fact, you paid for and are now reading a book that I have written, which is a manifestation of my love of writing. At the same time, it is not altogether necessary to demand that your creative, artistic expression become a way to make money. I have no desire to sell the few pieces of sculpture I have enjoyed molding. The feeling of working with the clay and seeing a form emerge is all I need. The act of doing it fulfills me. Perhaps you enjoy singing or playing a musical instrument. It should not be a necessity to perform in front of groups unless you want to. It is only imperative that you learn to know and love yourself by discovering delightful ways you can express your creativity in the physical world each day.

Does this mean turn off the television so you have the time to find out what hobbies, arts and experiences are fun for you? Yes, by all means, don't even bother to turn the television on. Certainly not every day and every night! A friend of mine had a delightful way of putting it. He said, "Turn off the television and Tell-A-Vision." It's probably time to quit living vicariously and begin to show your own vision, discover your own dreams and live your own experiences. Of course, you can watch television occasionally. There are some wonderfully entertaining and educational shows. I am just suggesting that in order to express yourself, you need to allow the time for discovering what you like to do.

Ask the non-expressive part-of-you who has limited your self-expression and believes you do not have talent or creativity "What are you doing for me by stopping my artistic ability?" Some answers might include:

- I'm staying free from risk.
- I'm avoiding failure. I can't draw a straight line with a ruler.
- I'm not artistic. I flunked my first grade art class.
- It's too much work to take classes and get out of the house.
- What does creativity have to do with making money?
- My family would think I am crazy.
- I might become lazy if I think I'm an artist.
- I get caught up in creative projects and don't do anything else.
- I might want to give up my job if I let myself become creative.
- Working hard is the best kind of self-expression.
- I'm not sure what I'd like to do creatively.

Add your own considerations.

Ask the non-expressive part-of-you "What if there were a way I could allow myself full self-expression and at the same time satisfy all the considerations you have mentioned? Would I be willing to change my behavior?" Send the non-expressive part-of-you to the creative part-of-you to discover at least three ways in which you can solve this problem and develop your self-expression. The statements that could change the negative position to positive are as follows:

- I can be free from risk and avoid failure.
- I don't have to be a creative genius. I can just have fun.
- My creative projects can be done easily and don't require a lot of time. I take classes if they are enjoyable.
- Equating money to creativity is not necessary, although my self-expression can be rewarded financially.
- My family will encourage me to express myself.
- I can relax if I want to and I will not become lazy.
- I can keep my job or find a new career that allows me to express myself creatively.
- I can make work into a fun and rewarding experience.
- I can discover what types of creative endeavors make me feel excited and fulfilled.

Complete the Infusion Integration Technique (see Chapter 12), bringing the two parts together to become one. Let your Higher Self flow love and light, healing and inspiration to all parts-of-you.

Now you are releasing your blocks to creativity. You are allowing the creative power of the universe to flow through you. I believe that the words "Created in the image of God" means we are endowed with the creative energy of God. The universal principle of the God force appears to be creativity. God is love expressed as creativity.

Therefore, the creative love energy is the most powerful tool that you can use in your lives. When you are using your creativity, you are tapping into your intuition, your inner knowing. You become inspired, in spirit, in God. As the creativity flows through you, you are healing your mind, body and emotions. You become one with the inner joy that will sustain you through all your trials and tribulations, for you are no longer alone; instead you are all one. All parts-of-you can join together and enjoy the freedom to express your creativity.

CHAPTER 18

Stories of the Mind

Bring out the life, the strength, the purity and unselfish love which you possess within yourself; they are your birthright. Come up, come up bravely. There is no death for you.

The Path of Devotion

This chapter may seem mystical and mysterious, but I feel it is important to let you know of some unusual experiences that have happened to me while working with the Infusion Integration Technique. You may look at these experiences in a number of ways so that the underlying concepts or theories are comfortable for you.

On a few occasions, when using the Infusion Integration Technique, visions or scenes appeared in my mind, accompanied by intense emotion. The experiences were unusual because even though I was in the story or event, which was appearing on the screen of my mind, these emotional pictures were not of this lifetime. The events seemed to be past life scenarios. If you believe in reincarnation, these pictures are easy enough to explain. However, if you believe that we have only one life on earth, one explanation may be that the mind can and does weave stories, pieced together from various movies, television shows and books we have read, to come up with an interesting scenario to explain a problem or event that we are experiencing.

Another possible explanation for these stories of the mind, which appear to be past life phenomenon, is to imagine that coded within our DNA might be all the experiences of our ancestors. Perhaps, not only the color of our eyes, skin and hair, our height and the size of our shoes are determined by our inheritance, but also the remembrance of events and activities that have impacted the lives of our great, great grandparents.

Whatever your explanation might be of seeming to remember a past life, it appears that thousands of people are having spontaneous remembrances, which seem to provide an opportunity to serve as analogies, metaphors or mythologies for the mind to make sense of an experience. It may be helpful to understand that these experiences need not be frightening, but may be very helpful in releasing emotional blocks which are stopping our progress. It is interesting to note that thirty percent of the population of the United States believe in reincarnation. I assume that this figure is so high because many people have experienced what seems to be glimpses into past lives.

The first time I had such a past life remembrance was in November 1977. My skin broke out in a red rash for no apparent reason. With the urging of my boyfriend, John, it seemed worth the time to try the Infusion Integration Technique to find out what a part-of-me might be doing for me by creating this rash. I chose my right hand to represent the part-of-me who did not want the rash. My left hand represented the part-of-me who had created the rash .

In a moment, my left hand closed very tightly into a fist. John playfully started to pull my fingers apart asking, "What's this all about?"

As the fingers started to open, I suddenly saw a huge flash of light in my mind's eye. It was like an explosion. I felt an intense surge of emotion and began to cry.

John was bewildered and asked me what was happening.

I looked in my mind's eye and told him I saw a picture. It was twilight. I saw a country landscape with rolling hills. In the distance I saw what looked like fireworks. I then realized they weren't fireworks; they were bombs lighting the evening sky. I heard explosions as they landed nearby. I noticed that I was sitting on a small hill, and a few feet away to my right was a hat, a wide-brimmed, metal hat which appeared to be a World War I helmet.

I started crying heavily as emotion swept over me. John comforted me and asked again, "What else is happening?"

Suddenly, I felt an intense pain in my legs. I looked down (in my mind's eye) and saw that my legs had been blown off. My skin was red and burned. I had stepped on a land mine. In this story I was dying. I then knew that I was a soldier in World War I fighting in France. I was about nineteen years old. What I was grasping so tightly in my left hand was a locket my girlfriend had given me. It had her picture in it. I cried with a deep sense of loss and sadness.

John stood over me, and as I quieted down, he again asked me what I was seeing in my mind's eye. I told him I saw myself floating among the stars. It was extremely beautiful. A sense of warmth and love bathed me as I felt at one with the universe.

A moment later, I saw myself at my funeral. I was experiencing the scene from the perspective of being lowered in a casket into the grave. I could see through the top of the casket and watched everyone looking down at me. My girlfriend and my family were crying. I saw my dog with the black spot over his right eye and ear peering over the edge of the hole.

A second later, the scene changed. I seemed to be surrounded in ethereal light as some people came to greet me. They said I would be spending some time in a hospital in this other dimension. I would learn over time that, in this other reality, I was not hurt, that I still had legs, and I would be able to walk again in my "light" body.

Going with them to the hospital was the last scene of that event I saw in my imagination. The tears subsided, and I was emotionally drained, but I felt as if I had lived through an incredible experience. Even now, when I think of that event, when it seemed that I died in World War I, the memory seems more real than many days in this lifetime. Other such remembrances or stories have become metaphors for change and have helped me to clear away emotional blockages. By the way, the skin rash, which was the red and burned skin in the story, disappeared within a few days.

Obviously, we have not scientifically proven whether we have one lifetime or many. The concept becomes a religious issue since there are millions of people whose religion does teach of reincarnation, and other religions do not. Yet perhaps for a moment, we could put aside all discussion of whether or not it is true that we live more than one lifetime. Maybe, we could instead agree that the mind can and does manufacture and live intensely many stories, real or imagined.

How many times have you felt your hands become sweaty and your heart begin racing during a scary movie (especially when the director catches you and the audience unaware)? The gasps, and sometimes screams, that come from the audience in the darkened theater, are elicited by imaginary experiences. You are watching light illuminating film, depicting images, moving in sequence in front of a camera. Yet you react as if the event is happening to you.

The point is: these are stories, whether they be past lives, compiled memories of our ancestors, or pieced together events from current life memories. They are just stories. And since they are just stories of the mind, you can change them. You can change the events if you don't like the way the main character, which is you, is feeling or experiencing the activities of the story.

Using this idea, I did go back in my mind and changed the World War I story. I saw myself running across the field, and I did not step on the mine. Instead, within a few days an armistice was called. I went home, married my girlfriend, had many wonderful children and lived a long and happy life. I created a new ending and changed the story, thus changing my emotional reactions, past and present. If you do want to entertain the idea of past lives, it is interesting to note what happened at the end of every lifetime. You died. Yet you are still alive. If the idea of reincarnation does not sit well with you, then the concept of stories of the mind still applies. You may have noticed that your mind is always full of stories. You are thinking about what someone said or did to you. Your thoughts are full of past experiences or future plans.

If it is possible to change the stories of your mind, this means you can change any memory you have gathered in this life. Perhaps you did not get invited to the big high school prom or go to the college of your dreams. You can go back to those events in your mind and change them. Because your experiences are just stories, similar to old videos, you can erase or tape over the events that bother you.

See yourself attending the prom and having a wonderful time. Watch yourself graduating from the college of your dreams and walking proudly with your diploma. If you were abused in your childhood, go back to your earliest memory and change it. See yourself loved and adored and treated as a precious child. Hold and comfort yourself, and let the child in you know you are always with him or her. Create a new childhood. See yourself living new teenage years with helpful, encouraging and adoring parents.

Does this mean you are lying to yourself? Is this creating an unreality in which to hide? I don't think so. You usually know what has happened to you. You may know all the events and activities that bothered you or some of your memory may be missing. Whether or not you have total memory doesn't matter. In the end, it is the act of forgiving and changing your emotional reactions to all negative events which helps you to live a joyful life.

Everything that has happened to you up to this moment is a story—pure and simple. They are all just stories. You have a video tape library of stories of your life floating in your mind. Perhaps it is time to reconstruct your life, creatively, with new pictures, stories and feelings to fill your mind.

One example (of the idea that every event is just a story) is to look at the amazing phenomenon of eyewitnesses at an accident. It is a known fact, proven over and over again, that each eyewitness may have a different account of the accident. Is it just because they are standing in different locations viewing the event? Not necessarily. Many times the eyewitnesses are standing next to each other, yet each has a very different story to tell. Why? Because they are viewing the event through the filter of their own memories. They are seeing the activities of their lives with their own particular focus. They are aware of different details due to each one's viewpoint or past experience.

Let's imagine that five professional people go to a party. What might they each see? The dentist observes everyone's teeth. The dermatologist notices people's skin. The optometrist looks at eyes and glasses. The interior designer can later describe all of the furniture, floor and wall coverings. The gourmet chef will be able to tell you about the food. They have all attended the same party, but their description of the event will be extremely different as you interview each one of them.

We are all viewing every event, scene, person and activity through the filter of our particular interests, ideas and beliefs. Therefore, if we look at those people or events with a new and different perspective, we may see things we haven't seen before. The mind is far more flexible than we have given it credit. We are able to change our minds, change our beliefs, ideas, concepts and the stories of our lives as simply as we change a word or paragraph in a computer. This process of change requires our attention and the intention of remaking our lives in the image of happiness.

A friend of mine once told me he believed that this beautiful earth is actually a planet of rest and relaxation. It is a place of peace and tranquility where we can learn to work creatively in form, and the purpose of this life is to experience ultimate joy. This is a wild idea when we observe how often our world seems to be anything but peaceful and tranquil. Yet if, for a moment, we could imagine that this concept is true, if we could act as if this is the planet for rest and relaxation, maybe we would take the time and effort to change our concept of reality and create what we desire, instead of what we fear.

CHAPTER 19

Prayer and Meditation

Meditation is time spent with God
in silence and quiet listening.
It is the time during which the Holy Spirit
has a chance to enter into our minds
and perform His divine alchemy.
What changes because of this
is not just what we do, but who we are....
With our prayers we invite Him in,
He who is already there.
With prayer, we speak to God.
With miracles, He responds.
>   —Marianne Williamson
>   *A Return to Love*

You have been on quite an adventure. You have defined your primary sub-personalities and written the new scenario of your life. You've met with your crew members and learned what they have been doing for you when they stopped the flow of manifestation or changed the course of your activities in ways that may not have been pleasing at the time. By using the Infusion Integration Technique you now have at your disposal a new tool that can help you update and change the beliefs, decisions and choices which no longer serve you.

Take a moment to visualize yourself once again on the square-rigged, sailing ship on which you started this journey. You are ready for your adventurous cruise. The crew has agreed on a course, and they have elected you to serve as captain, as long as you are able to maintain a peaceful, harmonious atmosphere on board.

So what is missing? You have the ship, an open sea, a destination, and a harmonious crew. What else do you need to move forward easily in your life?

You need the wind. Your ship needs the wind to open its sails, so it can float easily over the ocean of life. The ship requires the winds of nature to create movement.

You need the breath of God, Christ, the Holy Spirit, the eternal energy of life, which is within you, to move you toward your goals and to fulfill your heart's desires. You need this infinite force to create a peaceful atmosphere in your heart, which allows your life to be joyful as each day unfolds.

I have found that there is a tremendous power of transformation through the use of prayer and meditation. I do not believe the purpose of prayer is to beg Jesus Christ or the Lord God Almighty to provide our desires, for God not only knows, but is the author of the strong and purposeful desires of our heart.

We may not always know for certain what God desires for us, but a strong wish should be respected, for it may be the voice of God in our hearts urging us to move forward and grow in our lives. It can be helpful to pray for wisdom so we will be able to discern which desires are for the highest good of ourselves, humankind and the planet.

It is important to remember that your mission is not to try to force things into manifestation, nor to put pressure in a given direction. It is best not to decide that a certain thing must be done, or it must be done now. This type of force is using mind or will power. Will power may produce what you think you desire, but the events and things you create with mind power and force of will may not be the best manifestation for your highest good.

I suggest that you do not pray for things or events to happen, but to ask instead for awareness of what decisions or beliefs you hold that may be blocking your path. Pray that God's will be done. The nature of God is perfect, omnipresent, all powerful, good and boundless love.

When you ask for God's will to manifest in your life, you are asking for freedom, security and happiness. You are opening yourself to feel infinite love and to experience peace of mind. You are requesting the ability to share love and peace with others.

Practice praying for wisdom, love and peace. Open your heart and mind in meditation to the Holy Spirit, the indwelling Christ consciousness, and the love of God. You will then be able to relax and allow divine intelligence to work through you and help you make win-win, rewarding decisions and choices in your life. Meditation is taking the time to quiet your mind, silence your ego and listen to God.

Often, during meditation, answers to your questions do not seem apparent. The small, quiet voice or a guiding vision may not come forward at that time to inspire you as you sit quietly. Yet, in those moments of quiet reflection, you are learning to discipline your mind. You are gaining control of "mind wandering."

My guidance often comes to me when I least expect it—when I am taking a shower, brushing my teeth or driving the car. When I am mindless, free of worry and concern, then I am able to hear that quiet voice giving me a helpful thought or suggestion.

At first, this contact by your true self may be called intuition. Your intuition is often felt as a clear, concise, positive thought, which has a slight edge to it. The intuitive thought feels different from your everyday thoughts. It may have a feeling of "aha," and give you a sudden insight, which feels different from gathering information from the past. It feels inspired.

What often follows the clear intuitive thought is an argument orchestrated by your ego, such as: "Why should we do that? I don't understand what you mean." As you pray for inspiration, this glimmer of intuition begins to grow and strengthen. Eventually, this intuitive feeling can become a clear and definite sense of the presence of God within you.

The quiet you achieve as you practice meditation can become your normal way of being throughout the day. Your peaceful mind can resemble a lake which has become calm and mirror-like. The trees bordering the lake are reflected so perfectly that they look like mirror images of themselves. As your mind becomes peaceful and calm, the will of God, the highest form of inspiration and guidance, can be reflected in your mind. You can allow your highest purpose to grow and flow through you without the confusing thought patterns that often fill our heads with turmoil.

Your prayerful, meditative moments can expand, filling your life with peace as you contemplate the eternal and think about God. As you become more aware of the presence of God, the indwelling Christ, you begin to realize your continuous relationship with this holy presence. When you acknowledge this presence within you and relax into it, you are able to let confusion and doubt dissolve into the infinite love which is always available for you. In those meditative moments, you can allow yourself to release your pain and frustration, your fear and anger into the all knowing and always loving God.

Prayer, meditation and forgiveness are the most powerful tools you can use in creating a loving, peaceful and joyful life. As you turn your attention to Christ (or God), you allow your mind, body and spirit to form a holy unity. By learning to quiet your mind as you contemplate the infinite source of all love, you can become one with that source.

If it is true that God knows the true desires of your heart, then imagine that those desires and purposes are sitting before you hidden in a beautifully wrapped gift box. This gift is wrapped in gorgeous, multi-colored paper and is tied with a special silk ribbon. The way you can open this box is through prayer and meditation. By quieting your mind and opening to the universal power of God, you can know, appreciate, and live your highest purpose in life.

Learning to forgive yourself and others can be the most freeing experience of your life. I remember standing before a mirror, looking deep into my own eyes, seeing the pain and sadness staring back at me. I mustered all my energy to say to that person in the mirror, "I'm sorry for my mistakes, which hurt you so badly. Please forgive me." And I saw and heard myself saying, "I forgive you." I wept as I released the judgment that I had placed upon myself for making so many ridiculous mistakes and stupid decisions. I realized that everyone has made mistakes.

The difficulties and problems we have created were usually based on a need for protection, a feeling of fear. As we begin to understand that only love is real, we quit judging and can forgive ourselves and others, for often we know not what we do.

Writing your preferences, getting to know your sub-personalities, and using the Infusion Integration Technique will all help you in the process of knowing yourself. You will be able to unlock the mysterious power of creation as you release the beliefs and decisions which have been holding you back from your highest good.

The power of God is available to assist you lovingly every step of the way. May you feel the infinite love of God, the transforming grace of the Divine Spirit, and the forgiveness of Christ, creating a peace which passes all understanding.

CATCHING THE WIND

Waves, patterns of waves, swirling, interweaving patterns
moving past the ship, as you sail steadily
across an endless ocean.
Dancing dolphins play in the misty atmosphere,
reminding you to think lightly,
to relax in your reverie.

You are captain of your ship, master of your fate.
You are well meaning and aware
as you watch the horizon,
knowing in your heart the balance point,
that place of neutral where neither friend nor foe,
desire nor fear can threaten your peace of mind.

You are at last headed home on this floating dream.
catching the next wind to a destination unknown,
yet clearly imagined, relaxed in your journey,
not worried about outcomes.

Each port, each meeting place, is another opportunity
to learn, to grow, to look deep inside,
to refine and integrate who you are,
who you have been.

The clear sky and shimmering sea
are illusions of great depth.
One covers, the other holds you,
and both set you free to roam the emptiness,
to define the fullness, to explore infinity.

Verlaine

CHAPTER 20

Correlations

To help you use the Infusion Integration Technique, I have provided a list of events or feelings you might experience.

- Column one lists experiences/feelings.
- Column two lists possible underlying beliefs.
- Column three describes what the experience may be doing *for* you.
- Column four integrates the benefits of the problem with the desired result. These statements can become your new beliefs.

Your "underlying beliefs" and "what an event is doing for you" may be different from this list. Do take the time to ask the part-of-you creating the problem "What are you doing *for* me?" Listen closely. Then do the Infusion Integration Technique.

Experiences/ feelings	What are the underlying beliefs?	What 's this problem doing *for* me?	Integrate benefits with desired result.
Accidents	Life's dangerous. Accidents happen anytime. I can't handle problems.	Accidents give me time to rest, take care of myself and think about my problems.	I can take time to rest, care for myself and handle my problems without drama.
Arguments	The way to win my point is to argue. Communication is very difficult.	Arguments make me aware of opposition. Arguments help me to communicate.	I can learn from opposing viewpoints and communicate without arguing.

Experiences/ feelings	What are the underlying beliefs?	What's this problem doing *for* me?	Integrate benefits with desired result.
Concentration (Lack of)	I get confused with too much to do and too little time to complete it.	My mind wanders so I don't become bored concentrating on just one thing.	I can be aware of all I need to do and focus on one item at a time without being bored.
Control	I need to control everything for life to be smooth.	Being in control protects me from fearful experiences. Control keeps me safe from surprises.	I can feel safe and be spontaneous without fear. I can enjoy people and events that surprise me.
Depression	Life is difficult and not worth living. The future looks bad or empty.	Being depressed keeps me separate from people and away from problems.	I can feel safe and can handle people and problems now and in the future.
Disrespect	I'm unworthy. I'm not good enough.	Disrespect shows me my weaknesses. It keeps me humble.	I am worthy and can be respected for my skills and be humble.
Exercise (Lack of)	Exercise is painful; I am exhausted every time I work out.	Not exercising lets me take it easy and relax.	I feel better after I exercise and my body is vibrant and alive.
Exercise (Too much)	Exercise is important so my body will not fall apart.	Exercise keeps me fit, active, attractive and I don't have to think.	I can enjoy exercise and take time to rest and relax my mind.
Guilt	Past mistakes are always there to haunt me.	Guilt reminds me of my mistakes and my weaknesses.	I can learn lessons, live for today and forgive my mistakes.
Illness	Bodies are weak and open to disease. Illness is the only excuse for relaxing.	Illness helps me relax and lets me escape from problems, and I receive attention.	My body is strong and healthy. I can relax and receive the attention I need.
Loneliness	Being alone is a sign I'm not loved and no one wants me.	Loneliness makes me attend to myself and keeps me safe and free to think.	I can pay attention to myself and be free to think and share with loving people.

Experiences/ feelings	What are the underlying beliefs?	What's this problem doing *for* me?	Integrate benefits with desired result.
Loveless - Lack of a Personal Relationship	People are not trustworthy. Commitment means confinement.	Lack of commitment makes me independent and unbothered. I'm able to make my own decisions.	I'm committed, yet independent, and am able to trust as I make my own decisions in a loving relationship.
Money (Lack of)	If I'm rich, I won't be liked and people will be jealous.	Lack of money is an incentive to work harder and become stronger.	I can have wealth, be strong and be liked by sharing my money lovingly.
Powerless	Power is a corrupting force. I'm not worthy.	Without power I am good, kind, spiritual and humble.	I can use my power and stay humble by helping others.
Regret	You can't do or have what you want or need. Life's not fair.	Regret reminds me of what I've missed, so I'll live more fully.	I can live my dreams now and experience joy without regret.
Sexual Harassment; Innuendo; Abuse	The human body is a sex object. All men/ women are only interested in sex.	Sexual remarks make me aware of my sexuality. Abuse makes me want equality and respect.	I can be loving, sexually fulfilled, feel protected and be treated with equality, respect and dignity.
Sex (Lack of Interest)	Sexual activity is painful and bad. Sex is too much of a commitment. Sex is overwhelming and dangerous.	Lack of interest in sex keeps me strong and safe from becoming too close to another, and I stay out of trouble.	I can be strong and safe, yet close to another person. I can commit to a loving sexual relationship without danger.
Sexual Obsession	To be attractive I must have many lovers to prove it.	Sex gives me a feeling of being wanted and needed.	I can feel attractive and wanted in a relaxed relationship.
Theft	People are thieves, stealing your time and money. People want what I own. I can't trust what they say or do.	Theft creates discernment about people, making me protective of time, money and belongings. It keeps me on guard.	I can be discerning about people and know who and what is safe for me, my time, money and belongings.

Experiences/ feelings	What are the underlying beliefs?	What 's this problem doing *for* me?	Integrate benefits with desired result.
Weight (Over-)	I need extra weight in case I get sick. I must eat to live. If I gain power I must be bigger. I can attract attention if I'm overweight. Fat people are great comedians.	Extra weight keeps me healthy, strong and able to perform. Fat protects me from attracting unwanted sexual attention. I'm the life of the party because I'm funny and fat.	I can be slender, healthy, strong and able to perform. I attract only the attention I desire and can be the life of the party when I am witty, charming and slim.
Weight (Under-)	You can never be too thin. Food is bad. To be fit is to be thin.	Being thin makes me fashionable, sexually attractive (or it keeps sex out of my life).	I can be my perfect weight and be fashionable and have only the amount of sexual experiences I want.
Worthless	To feel worthy is to be pompous and overbearing.	Feeling unworthy keeps me separate, safe and working hard for approval.	I can be safe and feel worthy and I do not need to act pompous or overbearing.
Worry	There are so many things that might go wrong, I must think about all facets of my problems.	Worry keeps me aware of negative events that could happen in my life and protects me from upsetting surprises.	I can make correct decisions and feel safe from upsetting events without worrying about the negatives.

Notes

Notes

Notes